The Complete Book of
Jewelry Making

Carles Codina

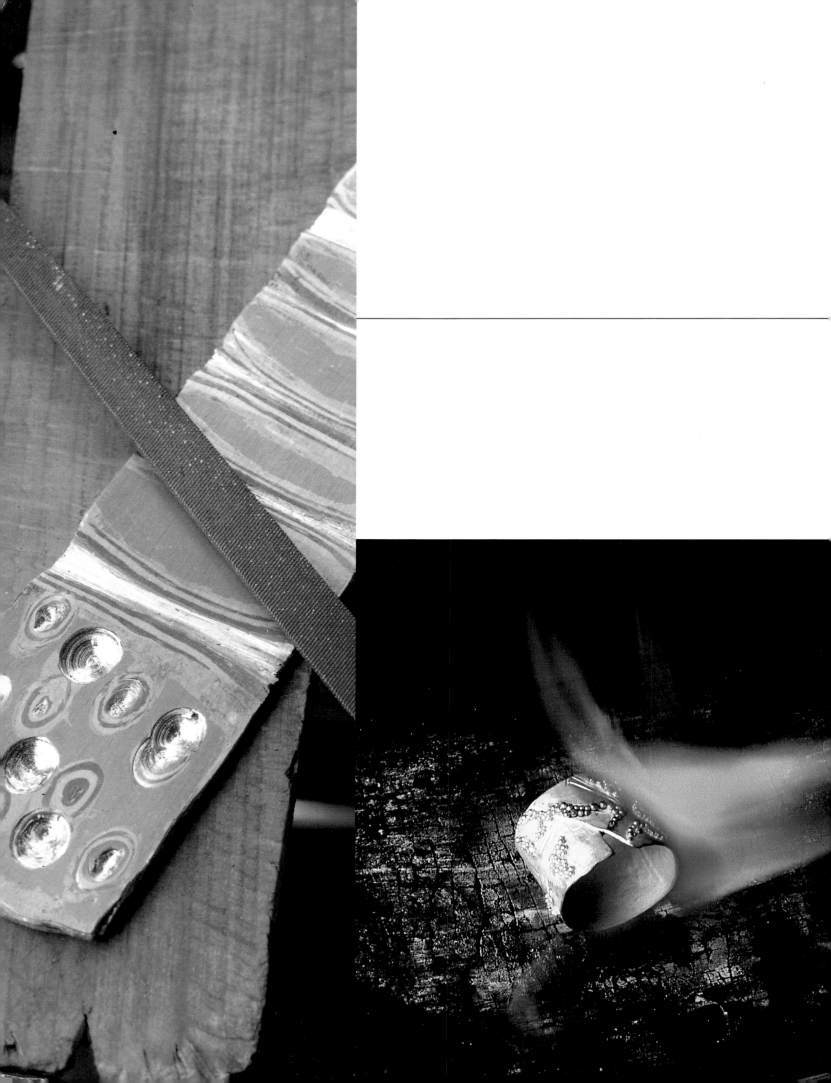

The Complete Book of
Jewelry Making

The Complete Book of Jewelry Making
Carles Codina

Editorial Direction: María Fernanda Canal
Texts and Coordination: Carles Codina
Other collaborators: Xavier Doménech ("The Origins of Orna-
mentation") Ramon Puig Cuyàs ("Contemporary Jewelry")
Projects by: Carles Codina, Estela Guitart, Carmen Amador,
Tanja Fontane, Aureli Bisbe, Ramon Puig Cuyàs, and Joan Avi-
ñó. Other collaborators: Jimena Bello, Verónica Andrade, Joa-
quim Benaque, and Jaime Díaz
Collection Design: Josep Guasch
Layout: Josep Guasch
Photography: Nos & Soto
Illustrations: Juan Carlos Martínez
Production Address: Rafael Marfil

Library of Congress Cataloging-in-Publication Data
Available

10 9 8 7 6 5 4 3 2 1

Published by Lark Books,
a division of Sterling Publishing Co., Inc.
387 Park Avenue South, New York, N.Y. 10016

Translation from the Spanish:
Laurie C. Jones

English translation © 2000, Lark Books,
Originally published under the title *La Joyería*,
by Carles Codina
© 1999 Parramón Ediciones, S. A.-World Rights
Gran Via de les Corts Catalanes, 322-324
08004 Barcelona (España)

Distributed in Canada by Sterling Publishing,
c/o Canadian Manda Group,
One Atlantic Ave., Suite 105
Toronto, Ontario, Canada M6K 3E7

Distributed in Australia by Capricorn Link (Australia) Pty
Ltd., P.O. Box 6651, Baulkham Hills,
Business Centre
NSW 2153, Australia

If you have questions or comments about this book, please
contact:
Lark Books
50 College St.
Asheville, NC 28801
(828) 253-0467

Printed in Spain
All rights reserved
ISBN: 1-57990-188-3

Introduction 6

Cont

Metallurgy 12

Basic Techniques 26

Surfaces 62

ents

Related Techniques 86

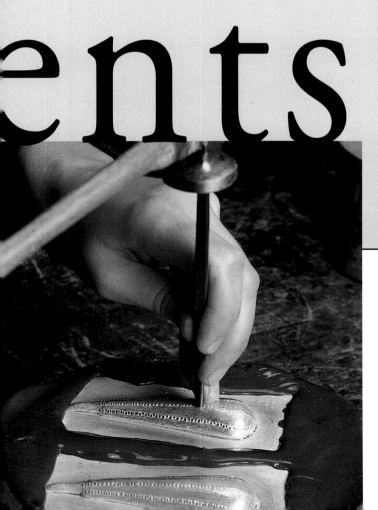

Step By Step 132

Glossary

Introduction

In the last quarter of this century many cultural values have come under scrutiny; among these has been the traditional place of the jeweler and the art of jewelry making. This has not, however, resulted in the rejection of traditional technique. On the contrary, techniques have been expanded upon and adapted to meet the expressive needs of today, even though the emphasis has been more on the use and application of jewelry than on technique itself. Contemporary jewelry embodies the qualities of expressiveness and provocativeness, and communicates the symbolic relationship with the object. These values are the same as those found in any contemporary art, and inherently demand the development of techniques which are increasingly more interdisciplinary and immediate, capable of being adapted to the needs of today. However, this freedom of technique and materials must be accompanied by sufficient artistic worth so as not to give the impression that "anything goes," a concept that does not necessarily have anything to do with correct technique.

Jewelry making is no longer defined, as it was formerly, by the type of metal used. Today, rather than a uniformity of style, we find a convergence of styles using a great diversity of materials and concepts. Jewelry can be created using any type of material that has the capacity to be transformed so as to achieve an expressive quality. This means that jewelry making techniques can encompass anything from works in paper to polyester, or joins made with anything from glue to rivets. At the same time, ancient methods, such as granulation or *mokume*, have been revived and reincorporated with enthusiasm, but in a fresh context.

Technological progress, applied to jewelry making, allows the artist a great deal of freedom. This progress is also fundamental to the development of aesthetic criticism, as well as to the establishment of formal criteria and aesthetic norms. Craft should be adapted to the expressive needs of the jeweler, who should not be made to feel limited by traditional critique of the craft. For this reason, the manner in which the craft is taught is very important, as is the role occupied by its schools and its instructors. This book attempts to give to the reader a range of freedom in decision-making and creativity. The different techniques demonstrated are meant to be flexible, to have immediacy—to be combined and changed—giving license to expression and symbolism. This book presents a great variety of technique and process. In doing so, it reflects what is entailed in teaching an art as old as jewelry making. It also reflects the future environment of teaching as one that allows for honest participation.

The teaching of jewelry making techniques, especially in a school of art, is usually the hardest part, appearing in many cases to be the antithesis of creativity. It is true that contemporary jewelry dispenses, in part, with traditional craft, due to the use of new materials and the introduction of new concepts. It is also true that the over-perfection of expertise, the drive for complete control over the materials, and the desire for excessive decoration, have played a major role in shaping today's image of the craft.

Jewelry making as we know it today exists thanks to the collective effort of humankind to contribute the necessary expression and sufficient substance to this art form. This book is the result of a collaboration with some of the best professionals in the field along with people just beginning in the craft. These include equipment manufacturers and art galleries; professors of jewelry making and their students; artists of other mediums; industrial manufacturers; professionals of classic as well as cutting edge contemporary work; plus others whose work exhibits such simplicity that no previous experience is required.

In summary, jewelry making is a passionate activity and its teaching has permitted the author to meet people who want to learn, understand, and share both the fascination of this humble craft and its advantages compared to many other such crafts; to understand what it means to feel the necessity of self-expression; and to know how to create your own personal world in a small space so reduced and miniaturized that, on occasion, it is capable of fitting in the palm of your hand. In a rational and demanding society where the relationship between an activity and its outcome is felt less and less, manual labor, and ultimately the creative process, allows one to create a tiny object that can then be shown off, put on, or given away—thereby both revealing and understanding one's self a little better.

Carles Codina i Aremgol has been an independent jeweler for most of his professional career, as well as a professor in the Jewelry Design Department of la Escuela Massana in Barcelona for more than 12 years. He has held various exhibits—both solo and group—of his work in Spain, Andorra, Holland, and Germany. He has also served as juror for a variety of jewelry design exhibits and competitions and as consultant for a number of local businesses and organizations.

The Origins of Human Ornamentation

Since time immemorial, albeit with varying intentions, the human race has adorned the body with ornaments. To speak of the origins of ornamentation is to speak of the origins of being human. The study of the history of human ornamentation provides us with a valuable instrument for reconstructing the history of human customs, traditions, and beliefs, as well as that of technological knowledge and aesthetic taste. Decorations and adornments are signs that communicate—instruments that have a function in themselves and possess a determined end.

During the Paleolithic period the function of pictorial representation was more magical than aesthetic. Its objective was to dramatize an event, a reality that was inevitably to happen. The Paleolithic artist was a hunter, and art was part of the magical skill of hunting. The artist didn't differentiate between fiction and reality, between the painting and the hunt. The only intention was to ensure the continuation of daily existence.

Human reasoning and learning relies heavily on classifying and grouping according to similarities, effecting changes and creating effects through mimesis. It is no surprise then, that the objects the Paleolithic artist used for adornment possessed magical characteristics which were related to their function. Shells, for example, because of their symbolic relationship to the feminine and fertility, were used to ensure pregnancy and the continuation of life. Other objects, such as teeth and feathers, were used to confer upon the wearer strength and energy. Being certain only of their function, we can understand that these objects were valued—considered, in fact, to be prized possessions, precious objects.

In Neolithic times, with the rise of farming and herding, human settlements first appeared and proliferated, accompanied by the interchange of commerce and trade. It was now possible for the first time to dedicate a certain amount of one's day to activities that had little to do with everyday survival. With the rise of a social order and the interrelationship between distinct groups, specialization in production emerged, along with a certain hierarchy of activity, especially in the organization of work. Social classes began to appear, as did the trades, among them the craft of jewelry. Social organization brought with it the recognition of needs never before experienced, such as aspects of morality and psychology, the confrontation of the individual with the community, and issues related to intimacy.

Socialization and organization in the Neolithic Age radically changed the values of the former Paleolithic Age. Rites and rituals replaced spontaneous magic. The hunter/gatherer of Paleolithic times did not rationalize his existence outside of everyday living. However, the farmer, the herder, and the artisan of the Neolithic period, sensed multiple possibilities in relationship to their destiny and believed that it depended upon intelligent and superior forces.

The worship of the sun and moon arose hand in hand with the idea of the unknown and the supernatural. It was the beginning of animism and the belief in an immortal soul. During the Neolithic Age, the first technical, socioeconomic, and religious foundations were established.

Beginning with the first civilizations and up to the present, the evolution of jewelry serves as an exceptional witness to the evolution and change of this age.

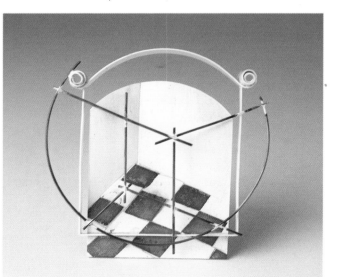

▲ Ceremonial knife, 12th c. Peru

▲ Each jewel is a fragment, a small chronicle of the great history of humankind.

▼ Brooch by Xavier Doménech, 1993

Contemporary Jewelry

The impact of the Industrial Revolution on European society during the second half of the 20th century is the context that gave rise to ideas such as those of John Ruskin and William Morris. These men denounced the machine and the division of labor as impediments to an authentic relationship between workers and their handicraft. With the mix of a new social ideal and a romantic vision of traditional medievalism, they proclaimed the worth of the artisan and art in everyday life. The ideals embodied in the English Arts and Crafts movement had a tremendous influence on the evolution of jewelry design, the applied arts, and industrial design throughout the 20th century.

In the last decade of the 19th century, these revolutionary ideas crystallized in a new international style that profoundly affected society and radically transformed the world of art—from architecture to jewelry design—and especially in the field of applied arts. Art Nouveau, Modern Style, Modernismo, Jugendstil, Sezessionstil, and Liberty are all different national expressions of a change that extended throughout Europe.

In the face of academic rigorism, a world of naturalistic ornamentation appeared, full of color, both linear and sinuous forms—where the motifs of flowers and vegetation, insects and birds prevailed, and where the feminine figure was usually central. For the first time in jewelry design, creativity and imagination were valued more than the materials employed, allowing jewelers much creative freedom; some pieces acquired the status of works of art.

The Sezessionstil and the Jugendstil movements followed William Morris rather than Paris *luxe*, extending their influence over all of central Europe, advocating a much more sober and austere style; emphasizing rationality, functionality, and clarity; and creating designs predominated by abstract motifs and simple geometrical lines.

Scandinavian artists, in particular Georg Jensen, from Denmark, introduced a new style with a much colder, more modern feel—works that remain classic today. Architects Josef Hoffmann, who worked with the Wiener Werkstätte, the center of arts and crafts in Vienna, and Belgian Henry Van de Velde, who considered it a moral obligation to create jewelry not for the elite, but for the general public, designed jewelry for mass production. Their designs not only heralded the coming of Art Deco, but also foreshadowed the dominate themes that appeared in the 1970s.

In 1925, Art Deco became the second greatest international movement of the industrial arts in the 20th century, of which jewelry design was a significant part. Since that time no other avant-garde style has had an influence of such magnitude on general society.

Alongside traditional jewelry craft mass-produced jewelry was being produced using the newest synthetic materials and industrial metals such as nickel, chrome, and aluminium—that clearly did not try to imitate precious metals.

▲ In 1895, the gallery Maison de L'Art Nouveau opened in Paris, housing objects in the Art Nouveau style, and demonstrating the strong influence of oriental art. During the 1900 Exposition, René Lalique converted Paris into the capital of jewelry design with the enormous success of his new collection of jewelry. Pectoral brooch in the form of a dragonfly by René Lalique

◄ Brooch of silver, malachite, opal, and coral by Josef Hoffman, 1903–1905

▲ Bracelet of chromed silver by Naum Slutzky, 1931

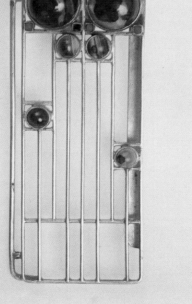

◄ Art Deco was expressed by rigorous technique and a geometric style that was clear and precise, giving preference to pure forms, rich but simple, without figurative elements. Brooch by unknown artist made of platinum, onyx, and diamonds

The outbreak of the Second World War interrupted a process that did not reemerge until the middle of the 1950s. The postwar period resulted in a generalized regression of the avant-garde spirit and a separation of the evolution of jewelry design from the rest of the arts. The idea that authentic jewelry is that which represents traditional forms and is made of precious materials was generally accepted by the most renowned of the major jewelry companies. It took several decades for these ideas to be influenced by changing social and economic conditions.

Jewelry as art began developing in the mid 1950s as a way of personal expression as much for the creator as for the wearer, reactivating the renovating spirit of the first part of the century.

The industrial and economic development of the 1970s resulted in the democra-

▲ Brooch of gold and diamonds by Reinhold Reiling, 1970

tization of consumer goods and the general introduction of social well-being, initiating from this period a redefinition of the social function of jewelry. Schools of art and design had a definite role in this renovation. The apprentice jeweler in a traditional workshop disappeared, to be replaced by schools of specialized, professional education. Schools of art came to be in charge of the formation of a new generation of jewelers. Such schools allowed an atmosphere of work and experimentation that was more

open to change and new influences, in contrast to the greater conservativism of more traditional workshops.

In this context—and under the influence of some of the ideas of William Morris concerning the worth of trades and crafts, and of the Bauhaus concerning the integration of design in industry—there came on the scene what is called contemporary jewelry, jewelry art, or jewelry design.

One of the schools that played a decisive role in the development of jewelry design in the 1960s and 1970s was Fachhochschule für Gestaltung Pforzheim of Pforzheim, Germany, directed by Karl Schollmayer, and including such professors as Klaus Ullrich and Reinhold Reiling. These professors called for the integration of jewelry design into contemporary artistic currents and the renovation of traditional techniques. Similar proposals arose in other schools, such as at the school Staatliche Kunstakademie Düsseldorf of Düsseldorf, Germany, with Friedrich Becker (known for his synthetic jewelry), Akademie der Bildenden Künste of Munich, Germany, with Hermann Jünger, and la Escuela Massana in Barcelona, directed by Manel Capdevila. These were later joined by other schools in Europe, the United States, and Japan.

Between 1950 and 1970, a group of Scandinavian jewelers stood out for their work dominated by the use of gemstones, simple forms, purity of line, and polished surfaces, especially in silver—such jewelers as Georg Jensen of Denmark, and Sigurd Persson and Olle Ohlsson, in Sweden. The Finnish firm, Lapponia Jewelry, with the designs of Björn Weckstrom, was a pioneer in showing that good design was not in conflict with industrial production or economic remuneration.

The second largest group was the German school that, despite its name, included artists of

▶ Brooch by Anton Cepka, 1991

many different orientations and nationalities. This group is distinguished for its use of geometric forms and complex structures, the use of nonprecious materials, and the clear desire to express one's individuality through the unique piece, an approach which permitted the development of the new jewelry craft in the shadow of industry.

Of important note is the work of the artists Bruno Martinazzi and Francesco Pavan of Italy; Anton Cepka of Slovakia; Peter Skubic of Austria; Gerd Rothman, Rüdiger Lorenzen, Claus Bury, and Manfred Bischoff of Germany; Max Frölich and Otto Künzli of Switzerland; the Dutchman, Onno Boekhoudt; Aureli Bisbe, Joaquim Capdevila, and Ramón Puig Cuyàs from Catalan; as well as a great many more who would comprise a never-ending list.

▲ Neckpiece by Hermann Jünger, 1979

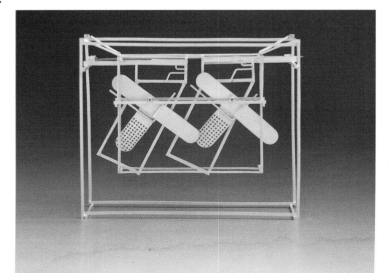

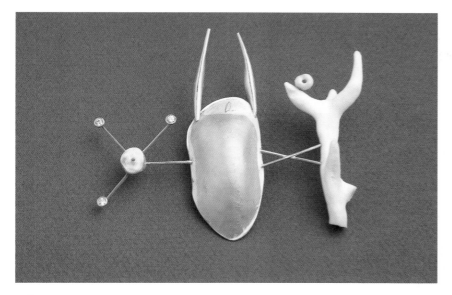

▲ Brooch by Manfred Bischoff, 1991

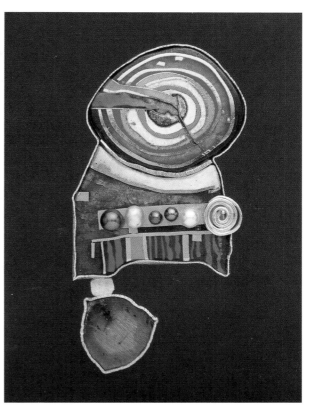

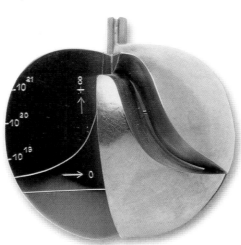

➤ Brooch by
Bruno Martinazzi, 1972

▲ In the United States a more eclectic style prevails, removed from the pure lines and predominating geometry of Europe. This style is distinguished for its figurative and narrative language, its variegated forms and symbols, and preference for the use of collage, of which Stanley Lechtzin and William Harper are two of the most distinguished artists. Brooch by William Harper, 1992

The new age of jewelry design has brought about a new and exceptional phenomenon. New artists are emerging from numerous departments of jewelry design from all over the world. The differences between them are diminishing as they forge together an increasingly international style.

Between 1980 and the end of the 1990s, conventional jewelry lost its reputation for ostentatiousness and wealth; instead a taste for simply but elegantly designed gold jewelry and precious stones became the norm.

At the same time, the creation of jewelry is divided into two very distinct cur-

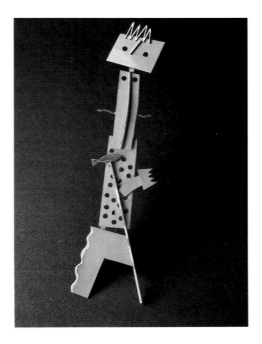

➤ Brooch made of oxidized and painted silver. *Arturus* by Ramón Puig Cuyàs, 1989

rents that mark the end of the 20th century. On the one hand, there is the production of designer jewelry oriented to the fashion world and to industrial design, and whose objective is to meet the demands of the market. Alternatively, there is jewelry committed to expressing universal values of art as a form of personal expression, which seeks a rapport with the wearer.

This is jewelry created more for its pure aesthetic pleasure than for commercial interests—jewelry making that attempts to mold the symbolic and spiritual values that have characterized the craft of jewelry from its beginnings—for a technological society confronted by the challenge of a new millennium.

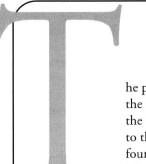

The progress of civilization is closely linked to the progress of metallurgy. Today, we study the remains of ancient civilizations according to the metal age within which they are found. Owing to its yellow color and durability, gold has been used in almost all known cultures.

The Latin word for gold, *aurum*, which means "brilliant aura," reminds us that for some civilizations it was thought to belong to the sun, and magical properties were attributed to it. The Egyptians buried their pharaohs with it to ensure safe passage to the other world. In the Middle Ages, alchemists and philosophers hypothesized means of converting metal into gold. Later gold was given curative powers that were eventually discarded with the passing of time.

This precious metal has always dazzled humanity. Wars have been waged and cities built in its pursuit. Gold's worth as a sign of wealth and power has been coveted by the majority of peoples and cultures since the beginning of human history, and its value continues to rise to this day.

Metallurgy

The Properties of Metals

Everything around us has a molecular composition, a combination of the 103 primary known elements that form the periodic table. Among these elements are gold, silver, platinum, copper, cadmium, tin, and lead. The elements of the periodic table, each assigned their respective symbols, are characterized by a particular structure, weight, and atomic number. When metals are mixed together, their characteristics change—they become more durable or soften, they change color, and their melting point increases or diminishes.

Gold and silver are the principal precious metals presented in this book. They are the ones we use in greater proportion with *alloys*. Alloys are responsible for changing the properties of precious metals when melted with them.

In order to make a metal that is hard and malleable it is important to know how its internal structure changes when it is subjected to significant changes in temperature and pressure.

At room temperature, metal is made up of a series of regular crystalline structures, naturally given to a certain order. The structure of metal can be compared to a beehive, which is formed by hexagons of wax superimposed upon each other to form the larger structure. There are seven systems of crystals, and within these, 14 lattice configurations. Some crystals have

▲ Metals in their pure state usually come in granular or laminated form.

cubic shapes and others have hexagonal shapes. The metals used in jewelry making (gold, silver, copper, nickel, lead, and aluminum) all have the same cubic crystalline structure.

When metal is melted, it changes from solid to liquid form, substituting its initial geometric structure for one less ordered and less geometric.

When metal cools it begins to regain its crystalline structure, but in a less ordered way, creating clusters that all have the same order but not necessarily the same orientation. More and more clusters form until they bump up against each

other. Lines or fissures form where the clusters meet. The smaller and closer the lines, the harder the metal. The crystals become limited in movement. Through laminating, forging, stretching, or whatever other metalworking process, these clusters become more and more compressed, reducing the free spaces and creating less room for movement. Hence, the metal becomes harder each time it is worked. When a metal is heated to its *annealing* temperature, it returns to a crystalline structure close to its original one. That is to say, it returns to a more ordered state and, by the same token, is once again pliable and easy to work. Applying heat accelerates the movement of atoms and subsequent recrystallization. This process is called annealing. In this state the metal contains small dislocations or spaces that permit more movement of the crystals and for this reason it is more malleable.

The manner in which the metal is cooled to room temperature is also important. If it is suddenly cooled in water, the reordering is interrupted. There are cases in which it is necessary to cool the metal quickly to conserve the structure of the crystals and there are other times in which it is not appropriate to do so, depending on the metal used and the temperature reached in annealing.

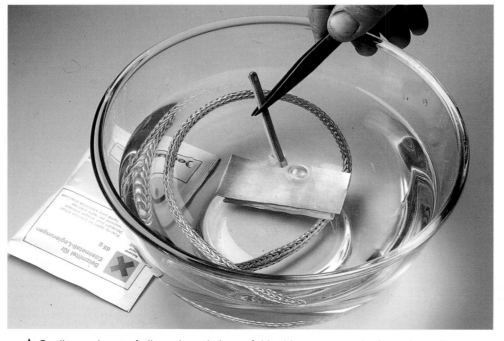

▲ Cooling an ingot of silver abruptly is useful in this case to make forged or rolled work.

Alloys

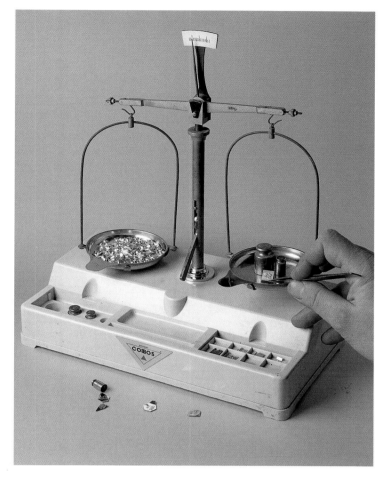

▲ A precision balance—an indispensable tool in the preparation of different alloys

▼ Since antiquity, jewelry makers and guilds have marked their work with imprinted seals that identified the artisan. Thanks to these marks we can catalogue and know their origin today.

Gold is one of the most malleable metals that exist, but without being alloyed it is much too soft. To give gold durability so that it can be worked into jewelry, it must be alloyed, that is to say, combined with copper, silver, or palladium, in order to make it more durable or to vary its hue to yellow, green, or white.

How to Calculate the Standard of Metal

Free of impurities or alloys, pure gold is said to be *1,000 fine* or 24 karats. The expression of fineness indicates purity. This can be noted in karats or in parts per thousand; they are both accepted units of measurement. The designation *18-karat* uses a standard of 24 parts; 18 parts are pure gold and 6 parts are an alloy. Fineness can also be expressed in parts per thousand, units of measurement which are much more precise and professional: 18-karat gold contains 750 parts pure gold and 250 parts alloy.

◄ Reliquary of Santa Cruz, Museo degli Argenti, Florence, Italy

Equivalents of karats to fineness	
Karats	**Fineness**
24	1,000
22	916
18	750
14	583
93	378
1	41.6

One karat is equivalent to 41.6 parts per thousand:

$$\frac{1 \text{ karat}=1,000 \text{ parts per thousand}}{24 \text{ karats}} = 41.666 \text{ parts per thousand}$$

To calculate how many karats are in a metal designated as 750 fine, divide that figure by 41.6 karats.

$$\text{Karats} = \frac{\text{fineness}}{41.6} = \frac{750}{41.6} = 18 \text{ karats}$$

Every country governs its standards of metals—an imposed minimum level of quality—which must be adhered to.

In a metals workshop, it is common to have metals of different origins, therefore making it difficult to know their standards. In such cases we highly recommend that you take a small sample to a specialized laboratory, whose analysis will give you a more exact result, expressed in parts per thousand. The next step is to raise or lower the purity of the alloy. Gold of a lower standard—for example, 583 parts per thousand (14 karats)—is raised by adding pure gold. On the other hand, gold of greater purity—for example, a gold containing 916 parts per thousand (22 karats)—is lowered by adding alloy. For both these processes, use the formulas that follow.

How to raise a lower standard using pure gold

The following formula converts a lower standard to a higher one by adding pure gold.

Formula 1

$$\frac{(\text{High standard - low standard}) \times \text{Weight of ingot}}{1,000 - \text{high standard}} = \text{Grams pure gold}$$

For example, to raise an ingot of 20 grams from 500 fine to 750 fine, add 20 grams of pure gold, as shown in this formula:

Example A

$$\frac{(750 - 500) \times 20 \text{ g}}{1,000-750} = \frac{5,000}{250} = 20 \text{ g pure gold to be added}$$

Adding 20 grams of pure gold to the original 20 grams of 500 fine results in a ingot of 18-karat alloyed gold (750 fine) weighing 40 grams.

How to determine the quantity of pure gold contained in a specific alloy

This formula calculates the quantity of pure gold in any given alloy by multiplying the weight of the alloy by its standard and dividing that figure by 1,000. The result is the quantity of pure gold and the difference is the alloy.

Formula 2

$$\frac{\text{Weight of alloy} \times \text{standard of alloy}}{1,000} = \text{Quantity of pure gold contained in the alloy}$$

Applying this formula to the above example (a 40-gram ingot 750 fine) the result is:

Example B

$$\frac{40 \times 750}{1,000} = 30 \text{ g pure gold}$$

The ingot of 40 grams of an 18-karat alloy (750 fine) contains 30 grams of pure gold.

Return to Example A and calculate how much pure gold is in the initial alloy of 500 fine in order to verify that the ingot of 40 grams of 18-karat alloy does indeed contain 30 grams of pure gold.

First, calculate how much pure gold is in the alloy of 20 grams 500 fine:

Example C

$$\frac{20 \times 500}{1,000} = 10 \text{ g pure gold}$$

The result is 10 grams of pure gold. Adding the 10 grams of pure gold contained in the alloy of 500 fine to the 20 grams of pure gold that was added in Example A, the yield is 30 grams of pure gold. This is the same result as in Example B.

How to lower a higher standard using an alloy

The following formula lowers a high standard by adding alloy to the metal.

Formula 3

$$\frac{(\text{High standard - Low standard}) \times \text{Weight of the ingot}}{\text{Low standard}} = \text{Quality of alloy to be added}$$

For example, to change 25 grams of 22-karat gold (916 fine) to 18-karat (750 fine), apply the above formula as follows:

Example D

$$\frac{(916 - 750) \times 25}{750} = \frac{4,150}{750} = 5.53 \text{ g alloy}$$

Adding 5.53 grams of alloy to the 25 grams of 22-karat gold (916 fine) yields an 18-karat ingot weighing 30.5 grams.

The term *karat* is used in reference to gold alloys. It is a measurement unit that is distinct and separate from the *carat*, which is used for precious stones. The carat is a unit of weight equal to 0.2 grams.

Gold	
Symbol	Au
Atomic Number	79
Atomic Weight	196.9
Density	19.3
Melting Point	1063°C

How to Determine the Karat of an Alloy

In a metals shop the most common method for determining the karat of an alloy is with the use of a *touchstone*. It's an easy method and frequently used to determine the karat of gold. However, it is not as precise as a chemical analysis done by an expert, which would indicate with greater precision the standard of the metal in parts per thousand.

First, rub the touchstone with the metal of unknown purity. Alongside this mark, rub the touchstone with an alloy of a known standard. Apply touchstone acid to the two marks and observe how they burn. If neither mark burns away then the standard of the metal is close to that of the known alloy.

For example, to determine whether a gold ring is 18 karats, first *file* down a place on the ring to eliminate the possibility that it is plated. Next, rub the touchstone with the filed edge. Right next to this mark make another mark with a metal that you know is 18-karat gold. Then put a drop of 18-karat touchstone acid on the two marks and watch to see if the first mark burns off. Burning indicates that the gold is inferior to 18 karats; if it doesn't burn, then the gold is equal or superior to 18 karats, but the exact standard is still unknown.

The touchstone acid method indicates with a certain imprecision that the metal is superior to the karat of the acid used because the gold didn't burn away. To know if the gold is of 22 karats repeat the above operation with an acid of 22 karats. If instead it burns away, repeat the test with an acid for 14 karats, and so on, until no burning occurs.

There are specific touchstone acids to test for silver content as well, but if we were to analyze them with 18-karat gold acid, the mark would turn light blue, reacting to the chloride in the silver.

▲ To test the karat of an alloy, rub the piece on a touchstone and apply touchstone acid of the same karat. In this photo, we rubbed a little silver and a little 18-karat gold and applied an 18-karat acid. The silver shows blue and the gold is shiny.

▲ The basic equipment needed for touchstone testing includes different acids, a touchstone, and a testing star. The most common touchstone acids are of 14, 18, and 22 karats. Each point of the star is made of a different purity of gold.

Silver

Silver is a highly malleable metal and, like gold, very soft in its pure state. It becomes more durable and resistant when alloyed with copper, but it also becomes more susceptible to tarnishing.

Silver is frequently alloyed with copper to render it 925 fine (that is, 925 parts pure silver and 75 parts copper).

Silver		
	Melting point	**Density**
Pure silver	960°C	10.5
Sterling silver 925 fine	893°C	10.4

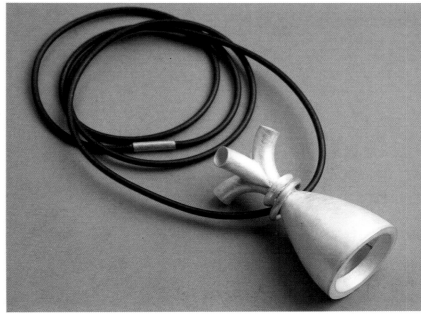

➤ Silver pendant by Xavier Doménech

Melting

It is essential to complete some basic calculations before beginning the alloying process. The most important of these is the calculation of the amount of alloy necessary for the required standard.

The alloy most commonly used in jewelry making is 18-karat gold (750 fine). To find the amount of base metal needed, multiply the quantity of pure gold you want to use by 0.33.

As an example, add 24.75 grams of base metal to 75 grams of pure gold in order to obtain the correct karat of the alloyed gold.

75 g x .33 = 24.75 g of alloy

The total weight is 75 + 24.75 = 99.75 g 18-karat gold.

Adding a quantity of alloy equal to 33.33% yields a gold precisely 750 fine, which meets the specifications of the 18-karat standard. Many metal refiners add only 32%, to obtain a slightly higher standard, especially if they use a centrifuge.

◄ Silver, copper, and flux are the three essential elements in the preparation of alloys.

▲ 1. The metal can be alloyed in different types of ovens. This is a gas oven with electric fans and an interior crucible.

▲ 2. Pouring molten metal into an appropriate mold form; here, a sheet mold is used.

◄ 3. To make wire, pour the melted metal into a wire mold. It is important that the mold be hot at the moment of pouring. If not, the metal will splash out due to thermal shock.

Yellow gold alloys	Metal	Fineness	Percentage
Green gold	pure gold	750	100.0
	silver	187	25.0
	copper	62	8.0
Straw gold	pure gold	750	100.0
	silver	125	16.65
	copper	125	16.65
Red gold	pure gold	750	100.0
	silver	62	8.0
	copper	187	25.0

▲▼ Tables A and B

Different palladium alloys used in white gold (in parts per thousand)			
Gold	Palladium	Silver	Copper
750	125	125	—
750	80	125	45
750	200	50	—
750	250	—	—

▲ 4. The cooled metal inside the mold is called an ingot at this stage of the work. The ingot should be pickled before being worked.

Yellow Gold

Eighteen-karat yellow gold is usually alloyed with a combination of half copper and half silver. According to the proportions, different colors and different hardnesses are possible. See Table A for the most frequent alloys used in yellow gold.

Increasing the ratio of copper in the alloy makes gold redder and harder, while more silver makes a softer, yellower gold. There are also prepared alloys available that give gold different characteristics and colors.

How to determine the amount of pure gold in an alloyed gold

For 18-karat gold, multiply the weight by 750 and divide by 1,000.

How to determine the amount of alloy metal

Multiply the weight of pure gold by 1,000 and divide by the purity of the alloy, in this case 750.

Converting the weight of a sample metal to the weight of gold or silver

$$\frac{\text{Weight of sample} \times \text{density of the metal to be alloyed}}{\text{Density of the sample}} = \text{Weight of the piece}$$

White Gold

Different alloys of white gold can be created by adding 250 parts per thousand of alloy containing different proportions of palladium, silver, and nickel. White gold has a very pale yellow tone and it is usually put in an electrolyte bath of rhodium after it has been polished. The preferred alloys are those which use palladium and silver (see Table B).

White gold (alloyed with palladium) is very soft and can be useful in forged pieces, but is not appropriate for wire stone settings or in anything that requires a more resistant metal. To alloy with palladium you need to use an oxygen-supplemented torch because the process requires very high temperatures.

Fluxes and Purifiers

After alloying it is important to use products that clean the metal and keep it from oxidizing. The most common product is *borax* because, when applied immediately, it eliminates surface oxidation and slightly raises the alloy's melting point.

Other fluxes that give excellent results are table salt, sodium nitrate, and potassium nitrate (saltpeter). Sodium bicarbonate is used especially to clean and purify filings.

▼ Earrings of white gold by Giampaolo Babetto

Annealing and Pickling

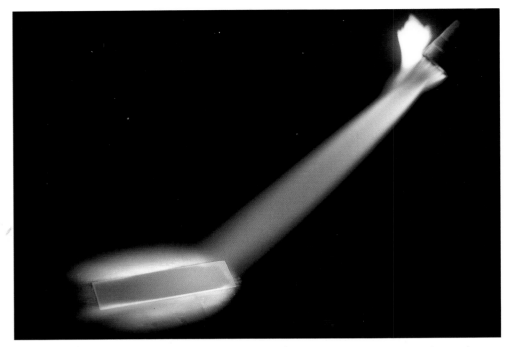

▲ Usually a soldering flame is used to anneal; applying uniform heat anneals the entire piece evenly.

Annealing and *pickling* are two very important processes in jewelry making. One does not exist without the other, and they must usually be done several times, especially in forged or rolled work.

Metal worked by mechanical means becomes hardened and requires annealing. This annealing in turn generates surface oxidation that must be stripped off by pickling.

Annealing

Metal gets increasingly harder as it is worked and may eventually crack or split and so must regularly be annealed. This process consists of heating the metal to its *annealing point.* This is the point at which the metal begins to return to a crystalline order close to its original and once again becomes malleable. It is also important that the annealing temperature is not excessive because this can produce internal crystals that are too big. However, if the temperature is not hot enough, the crystals will not reach a suitable size.

Not all metals *anneal* at the same temperature, nor in the same amount of time. It is usually unnecessary to anneal pure gold, but an alloy of 18 karats needs at least one annealing.

Annealing over a block of charcoal is recommended. This method reduces oxidation and enables you to more clearly see the reddish color indicative of annealing. It must be maintained at this color for some seconds before allowing it cool.

Each metal has its own particular annealing temperature and time. It requires some practice to correctly identify the dark reddish color that it should reach in the annealing process.

You can also anneal in an oven that has a good temperature regulator. In the case of straw gold (which contains 750 parts per thousand of pure gold, 125 parts of silver, and 125 parts of copper), once reduced to 75% of its original thickness, it is best annealed for 30 minutes at 550°C. However, in many artisan workshops it is not possible to work with an oven; even so, it can sometimes be more trouble than it is worth because the piece must be annealed many times as you work it. A quicker and more practical method is to use a torch on a work table. As the metal cools, you can interrupt the ordering of the crystals abruptly. This effect is good in some cases, but in others it is counterproductive.

Recommended annealing temperatures	
Metal temperature °C	
Copper	600–700
Gold	600–750
Pure silver	300–700
Platinum	600–1000
Standard silver	over 750

▼ For more uniform heating use pieces of natural charcoal and indirect heat when annealing wire.

When a work in progress or a sheet of metal is being worked, for example, the abrupt change of temperature can deform it. Water is best for the rapid cooling of metal. Use acid cautiously, as it produces toxic vapors and will burn clothes and skin.

Anneal standard silver rods at a substantially high temperature (more than 760°C) and cool with cold water.

A sheet of silver should be annealed, but at a lower temperature than for a ingot. Don't *pickle* it until after it has cooled to a temperature of less than 500°C. This prevents deformities.

No general rule applies to gold since its alloys vary, both in the quantity and type of alloys used. However, sometimes a sudden cooling softens gold more than a slow cooling.

Recommendations

When annealing a substantial amount of gold wire or very thin silver, accidental melting can easily occur. To avoid this, wet the wire with an anti-oxidant, and put them in an old can with some charcoal. Apply heat with a torch to the outside of the can. This allows for uniform heating and keeps the wire from melting.

An alternate method involves using a copper container with charcoal. Put the wire inside the container so that it doesn't touch the sides. Pre-heat an oven to the wire's annealing temperature and then place the container inside.

To avoid *oxidation*, use an anti-oxidant. This forms a film of salts that prevents the oxidation of metal when it is in contact with the flame.

Pickling

After alloying and annealing, a layer of oxide is formed on the surface of the metal, caused by the reaction of the copper in the alloy to oxygen in the air. Along with the oxide, there are also the scraps of *flux*, soldering liquid, or borax used in alloying. These must be stripped off. If left on, they will destroy the finish, and the metal will be difficult to *solder*. To do this, use a solution called *pickling acid*.

▲ Ingots in a pickling solution of sulfuric acid. Lead containers are impervious to heat and breakage.

A 20% solution (a one-to-five ratio) of sulfuric acid in water is commonly used for pickling gold and silver. This solution should be heated to be most effective; a cold solution takes much longer to strip the metal.

Safety Precautions

Always add sulfuric acid to cold water; it produces a dangerous reaction when added to hot water. <u>Never</u> add water to acid; always add acid to water.

Sulfuric acid vapors are harmful. Always use in a well-ventilated place. Splattered acid burns clothes and skin; use appropriate protective gear.

Other Pickling Solutions

For silver, copper, and brass, a solution of 10% sulfuric acid produces the best results.

For bronze, use a solution of *nitric acid* and water in equal parts. Use only for a few moments to take off the first oxidation, as nitric acid quickly begins to dissolve bronze. For subsequent picklings, use a 20% solution of sulfuric acid.

For gold, use a solution of one part nitric acid and 19 parts water.

Sulfuric acid solution is the most common pickling solution used in jewelry making, but because of the dangerous vapors it produces, consider the following alternatives:

A heated solution of 10 to 20% potassium alum dissolved in water produces excellent results.

Despite its disagreeable odor, the juice of one lime and sea salt in a copper bucket will strip oxide when brought barely to a boil.

There are other, less aggressive solutions than sulfuric acid used to pickle metal; these are especially recommended if your workshop is not adequately ventilated. They are commercially available from the manufacturers of jewelry-making chemical products and give excellent results when dissolved in water.

Do not put iron or steel in acid solutions. Remove objects from the pickle pot with tongs made of plastic, copper, or other non-corrosive materials.

After pickling, always rinse the piece with water and dry it before continuing work.

Removing Residual Acids

Salts neutralize acids. After taking a piece out of the acid, rinse it in a light solution of baking soda. This also helps to thoroughly remove acid from the interior of a hollow piece or a piece with a complex shape.

The Care and Recovery of Metal

Use alloying metals with the highest degree of purity. Take good care of your crucibles. When melting in a new crucible, prepare it by melting borax or a flux inside the crucible. Coat the walls of the crucible with a protective layer of the flux. The metal then flows more easily when poured.

Before melting them, sort leftover scraps from the scrap tray since all manner of material falls into it. Separate the filings, the scraps that are free of solder, and those that still have solder on them. Clean scraps can be melted as they are, but first pass a magnet over them to take out any bits of iron.

➤ Turn the crucible so that the flux completely coats the interior.

▼ The crucible is ready for melting.

When the filings are very dirty—when there is a great deal of solder on them, for example, or they contain particles of tin or lead—it is best to have them refined by a professional refinery. It is inexpensive, and avoids later problems with maintaining the purity of an alloyed metal.

When melting the filings, heat them in a pan or any other appropriate container, and then pass a magnet over them to take out the iron scraps. If the filings are gold, put them in a strong solution of nitric acid to eliminate copper, silver, and brass. When the reaction of the acid stops, which can take several hours, drain the acid from the filings, or empty them into a bath of distilled water. They can be melted using a mix of equal parts borax and baking soda.

The manner in which filings are melted is important. Mix a fairly large quantity of borax and baking soda in the crucible so that it produces a liquid, molten slag. This allows the small particles of metal to settle at the bottom of the crucible, rather than

remaining suspended. Stir the metal gently with a graphite rod. After alloying, it is advisable to have the metal analyzed to be sure of its purity.

When working with precious metals it is important to avoid some metals and harmful materials that, when mixed in the crucible, contaminate the new alloy.

Avoid contact with metals such as lead, tin, and aluminum as much as possible when working with gold or silver. As little as one gram of lead can contaminate as much as a kilogram of gold. The gold may be recovered, but not without a reduction, or *loss*, in weight from the original mass.

When working at the jeweler's bench, make sure none of the above-mentioned metals falls into the scrap tray. Suppose you are melting gold, and a piece of tin, for example, falls unnoticed into the crucible. The accidental combination of gold with tin will create small, visible fissures as the metal is rolled out. It will crack and cannot be worked. The state of the metal is *contaminated*, and it is one of the worst problems with which jewelers must contend.

▲ Small pieces of iron from jeweler's saws, files, and pieces of broken burs usually fall into the scrap tray along with tiny scraps of precious metals called filings. Use a magnet to extract any iron.

▼ Reaction produced by nitric acid when it dissolves metals such as copper and silver

▲ Contaminated gold

Small fissures appear in contaminated gold when it is rolled. The metal is cracked and is impossible to work with. You can sometimes tell if a metal is contaminated by the sound it makes when dropped on a hard surface. It has a deeper sound than when it is in good condition.

Refining

This is an easy and economical method, used since antiquity in small workshops, for separating gold from its alloy and extracting harmful metals from contaminated gold.

The process consists of alloying the gold that needs refining, at a ratio of one part gold to four parts copper. Once melted, roll it to a thickness of approximately .3 mm and cut it into pieces about 1 cm square. Submerge the squares in equal parts nitric acid and water to keep the acid from splattering. When the acid reaches the point at which it stops boiling, even when you add more acid, then the reaction is finished. Pour out the acid solution and add distilled water. When the gold is dry it is ready for melting.

◄▲ Always refine metals in a well-ventilated space using a respirator and special gloves.

Safety Precautions

Boiling acid emits nitrous vapors that should never be inhaled; also avoid any skin contact.

Always refine metals in a well-ventilated space using a respirator and special gloves.

Keep acid bottles in a safe place out of the reach of children, such as in a locked cabinet.

In case of an accident, wash the affected area with plenty of water and seek immediate medical attention.

Loss

When making jewelry, small pieces of metal are lost in the process. Much of this loss happens during alloying due to the splattering caused by excessive heat. These tiny splattered particles adhere to the sides of the crucible, but they are recoverable. Alloying and annealing produce oxides in copper alloys, and oxidation causes metal loss. Pickling also causes a small reduction in the weight of the metal. Use flux when annealing to reduce loss. Flux also leaves the surface of the piece in good condition,

Although effective in many cases, refining does not completely eliminate lead and other metals. It will be close to, but not exactly, a perfect 1,000 fine. Once refined, get a precise analysis of the metal's fineness. Don't use this gold in a 33.33% alloy because the fineness will fall below 750 parts per thousand; use a 32% alloy instead.

Extremely contaminated gold or an accumulation of filings can be taken to a professional refiner of precious metals. A professional refiner can refine gold with minimal loss.

➤ Using good polishing equipment with a vacuum and an enclosed motor helps control harmful dust. Machines equipped with a retrieval bag can help recover valuable precious metals.

▲ A jeweler's bench has a unique design that allows one to recover metal filings in a special drawer beneath the bench pin.

preventing *firescale*, or *firestain*, which often appears during polishing.

Filing, sawing, and polishing also cause loss. All of these create metal-laden dust which can never be completely recovered. Use a polishing machine that has an enclosed motor and a scrap tray; when cleaning out the retrieval bag, brush the gold filings from your tools and your arms.

Perhaps the most loss is generated by the polishing machine. Vacuum equipment can recover the scraps from the polishing paste.

Save all liquids—electrolyte baths, ultrasonic cleaning fluids, even the water you use to wash your hands—for the recovery of the metals they contain. There are special filtering sinks on the market for this purpose.

Waste

It is best to take your waste to a professional refinery since the recovery of certain metals is much too complicated a process for the average small workshop. Waste recovery requires the installation of appropriate safety equipment as well.

Always maintain a high standard of cleanliness and sort workshop waste appropriately to help facilitate your work. Keep several containers handy for sorting different types of waste. In one container, put the polishing paste and all material that has come into contact with metal such as leather polishing sticks and trash swept up from the floor. In another, put the scraps collected from the polishing brush and everything related to the buffing machine. In a third, put the waste from the crucible and the alloying process. In a small work-

shop where there isn't much waste, it's sufficient to have one container for all solid waste and separate only the liquid waste: the liquid from electrolyte baths should be kept separate from those which you use to wash your hands, other kinds of cleaning, or that are used in ultrasonic cleaning procedures.

To most efficiently reduce the volume of waste, burn it in a contained ventilated space so that the precious metals don't disperse. This considerably reduces the cost of recovery from a professional refinery. Be sure to check with your local regulatory agency regarding the safe disposal of heavy metals and toxic materials.

Basic
Techniques

Once you have mastered the elemental principles of metallurgy and alloying, you are ready to begin a series of processes that will allow you to advance in technique and, more specifically, in the processes that constitute actual metalworking.

The work of a jeweler includes rolling shapes, drawing wire, incising, forging, and soldering elements of construction. These processes are essential, and while it is not always necessary that they be executed exactly as described in this book, they must be mastered, as they represent the fundamental basis of the craft. While some of these processes appear simple and elemental, such as filing correctly, their proper execution unmistakably influences the result of the piece. They merit, therefore, the same attention you would give to the most sophisticated of techniques.

Each of the following sections contain step-by-step instructions and photos that describe these basic techniques. The last three sections demonstrate advanced techniques, such as linkages, closures, and rings.

Preparing Basic Shapes

Before beginning any work of jewelry, you must make an ingot into a specific shape. The shapes that are presented in this chapter are the most elemental: sheets, wires, and tubes. Once the shapes are prepared, you can begin such processes as sawing, soldering, or *forging* to construct different pieces.

Shaping metal subjects it to a great deal of pressure, which deforms it considerably and changes its internal structure. It is important to anneal the metal regularly—every time it reaches a reduction of no less than 50% of its initial volume—otherwise it loses its malleability. Cracks will form and it will ultimately break.

After annealing, the metal acquires surface oxidation that must be eliminated with pickling acid. After stripping the oxidation, rinse the piece well in running water, or add a little baking soda, in order to completely eliminate the remains of the acid. Once the metal is dry, it is ready to *roll* sheets or *draw* wire.

➤ Gold piece belonging to the Tolima civilization, one of the first civilizations that worked with gold found in rivers

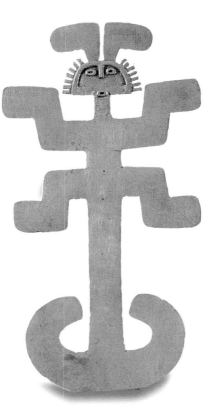

◀ Ring of silver wire by Xavier Doménech

Rolling

Rolling mills are essential pieces of equipment used to prepare different shapes. Rolling mills can make two types of shapes: sheets or squared bars, the latter being an essential first step to drawing wire. The sheet is one of the most basic shapes and can sometimes be found prefabricated in different thicknesses from suppliers of precious metals. It's a good idea, however, to know how to prepare sheets and wires yourself since in many cases they cannot be bought commercially. It's also useful knowledge for the recovery of metal scrap, which can be melted and rolled into new shapes.

To use a rolling mill, turn the crank approximately half a turn each time you insert the metal into the mill. Maintain the malleability of the metal by annealing and pickling as needed while creating the desired shape.

▲ The operation of a rolling mill is easy. Each time you make a smaller shape, turn the control handle a quarter to a half a turn, according to the type of mill. Insert a bar in the channel and roll it through by turning the handle a half-turn, or until the mill cannot close any further. Repeat this process using smaller and smaller channels to reach the desired size.

◀ This squared bar will be progressively reduced by placing it in smaller and smaller grooves. Its diameter is reduced a little more each time until it reaches a size that allows it to be drawn with a drawplate and tongs to make a wire.

▲ Once the metal has been alloyed, poured, and cooled in a mold and after it has been pickled, cleaned, and dried, it is ready to be milled. To do this, roll the ingot until it has been reduced to more than half its initial thickness, then anneal it in order to maintain adequate tensile strength and malleability.

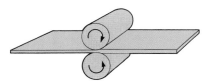

▲ To avoid cracking the sheet or rod during the rolling process, always roll in the same direction or the metal will break. If the direction is changed in order to obtain more width from the piece, anneal it first.

➤ The mechanism of a rolling mill is very simple. It reduces the thickness of the sheet as it is drawn through the mill by turning the control handle or lever, moving the top roll up or down.

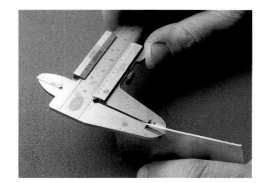

◄ Take measurements frequently with a gauge to check the reduction until you reach the desired thickness.

Drawing Wire

With a rolling mill you can make a rod of gold or silver, which you can then use to make wire. Draw the wire with draw tongs using a wire *drawplate* that forms and elongates the wire, giving it its final shape.

If you buy a wire drawplate, make sure it is good quality steel, because with continued use the holes enlarge and lose their original size. Also make sure that there isn't much difference in size between one hole and the next. The wire passes through with such force that great differences in size can cause the wire to break.

Anneal the wire after every fifth or sixth draw through the plate. Waxing the wire helps it draw with more ease.

▲There are four basic shapes in which to draw wire: round, square, half-circle, and rectangular. Because the most commonly used shape is the round, purchase two round wire drawplates, one with holes up to 1.5 or 2 mm and a larger one with holes up to 6 or 7 mm in diameter.

◄ A multitude of different wire drawplates with various shapes and sizes are available commercially.

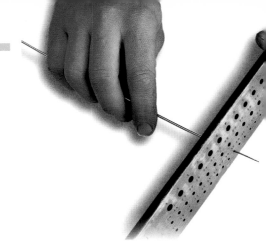

◄ 1. After rolling the bar, make a point on one end that is small enough to insert through the largest hole in the wire drawplate. Do this with either a coarse file or with a hammer. With the draw tongs, seize the point and draw the wire through the draw plate. For each successive pass, first reshape a smaller point.

▲ 2. Insert the point of the wire through the hole of the drawplate.

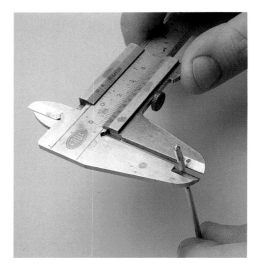

► 3. Draw the wire to the size and shape you wish to use. Seize the point of the wire with draw tongs and turn the crank on the side to stretch the wire. Do this so that the wire passes through a succession of smaller and smaller holes until it reaches the desired size.

▲ 4. By reducing the size of the hole, the wire will get thinner and thinner. Control the reduction by taking regular measurements with a vernier caliper.

▼ The different phases of reduction, from a bar of melted silver to a smooth round wire. The quality and condition of your wire drawing equipment are factors that will definitely influence the success of the final product.

▲Wire brooches by Christoph Contius

Making Tubes

The tube is an important shape because it is a basic element in many types of construction, such as hinges or stone settings. Since tubes are formed from sheets, it is essential to master the technique of soldering (fully discussed on page 42).

Making a tube is a simple process that requires a *grooved forming block* and a *cross peen hammer*, also known as a *jeweler's* or *goldsmith's hammer*. The edges of this type of hammer are rounded so that no marks appear on the tube.

Formulas for Cutting the Sheet

To cut a rectangular sheet correctly, it is important to know the width needed to create the tube's diameter. Use the following formula to calculate the width of the sheet when the exterior diameter is known:

> Exterior diameter - thickness of sheet x 3.14 = width of sheet to be cut

If only the interior diameter is known, for example, when fitting wire inside a tube, use the following formula:

> Interior diameter - thickness of the sheet X 3.14 = width of sheet to be cut

Closing the Tubes

After annealing the sheet, use a shaping block, and hammer the sheet along its interior side. Shape it uniformly, holding the hammer from the very end and striking it along the length of the sheet so that it bends slowly toward the interior and forms the shape of a "U".

The rounded edges of the cross peen hammer are important, but so is the width of the flat side of the hammer. This side should be slightly convex with no sharp edges. Make sure it is well polished because the texture of the hammer transfers to the metal.

Once you have closed the tube, draw it through one or two holes of a wire drawplate to give it better shape. Anneal the tube to keep it from opening when you solder it. This is very important with a large tube because it is *work-hardened* after being hammered. Sometimes the tube will open during annealing. If this happens, strike it with a hammer on the exterior side, and finish closing it before soldering.

After soldering, file off the excess solder and draw as you would a wire.

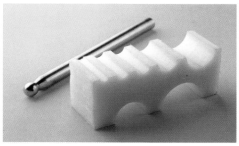

◄ 1. To make a tube or hinge, first start with a flat sheet, and cut a triangular point at one end with bench shears.

► 2. Next, use a cross peen hammer to close the sheet little by little on a shaping block. The blows are now on the exterior side, so use the flat side of the hammer, forming a round tube with the sides of the sheet coming as close together as possible for soldering.

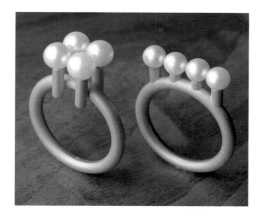

▲ Wire ring with tube supports for pearls. Work by Ulla and Martin Kaufmann

▼ Different types of hammers used in jewelry making

◄ The use of wooden shaping blocks is common. You can also make one from a block of nylon—drilling holes in a block and then cutting through the exact center of the holes.

◄ Stages in the making of a tube

➤ Different sizes of tubing

Ring of Bent Tubing

In many instances it is necessary to bend tubing, but the interior must be filled or it will be deformed. Various filler materials, such as plastic or special plasters, may be used as long as they resist pressure. With silver you can use a filler of aluminum, but extreme care must be taken when removing the filler, because aluminum pits silver if the metals touch during heating.

Copper is used to fill a gold tube because it dissolves easily in nitric acid. However, a metal worker should take necessary precautions in this instance, providing ventilation, using gloves and eye protection, and diluting the acid with water.

Making a ring of hollow gold allows for a more thorough explanation of tubing. You will need a gold sheet .6 mm thick and a square-shaped copper wire. Both should be annealed and pickled.

▲ 1. Prepare a sheet of gold and a square-shaped copper wire, as demonstrated on pages 28–29. Form the sheet into tubing on a shaping block, and draw the tube through a drawplate once or twice so that the squared wire fits loosely in its interior. Once the copper wire fits in the tube, you may solder the edges of the tubing immediately or wait until after you draw the two together one more time.

◄ 2. With the copper inside the tube, solder the edges of the tube so that the solder join is positioned over one of the corners of the squared wire.

➤ 3. Next, draw the two metals in a square wire drawplate, making sure the solder join lines up with a corner of the square hole. Draw them so that the copper interior fits tightly inside the gold outer layer.

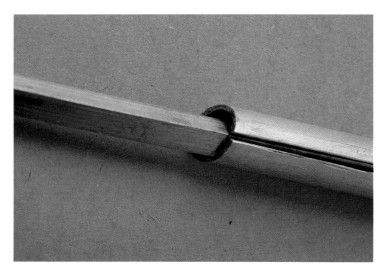

➤ 4. Shape the tube into the form of a ring. In this case, we used a ring bending machine, but you can also use a ring mandrel. You can even gently beat the tube into shape with a hammer because the copper interior will prevent it from deforming.

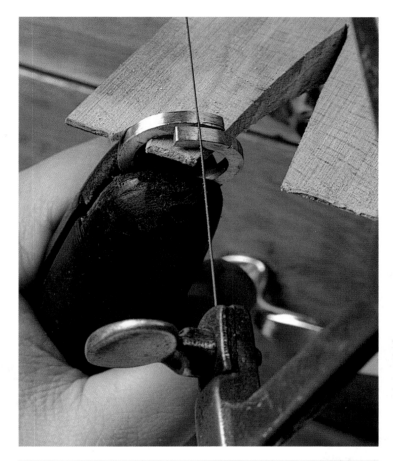

◄ 5. Once the ring is formed to the desired size, secure it in a ring vice and cut it with a saw, making the cut as straight as possible.

◄ 6. Hold the ring with two parallel pliers. These allow you to hold the piece along its surface without deforming it. Taking great care, bring the two ends closely together, and then once again saw through them to leave them clean for soldering.

▲ 7. Tie the ring with steel binding wire to keep it from opening when heated and creating a gap. This is likely to occur because the bent ring is under tension.

➤ 8. Once the ring is soldered and leveled, file out two curves on both sides of the ring to accommodate the wearer's fingers. In this case, we are filing the gold and the copper interior at the same time.

◄ 9. Before soldering the two gold caps, remove the copper interior by putting the ring in a bath of nitric acid. This will dissolve the copper without hurting the gold. Next prepare two small sheets curved on a forming block to cap the side openings.

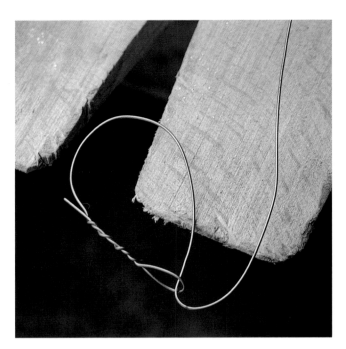

► 10. To secure the caps, tie them to the ring with binding wire. They should be well tied, but without excessive pressure that could deform the ring.

▼ 11. Cover all prior solder work with a solder inhibitor to keep the flame from remelting it. You can use yellow ocher mixed with water, or a commercial product made specifically for this purpose, as we did here.

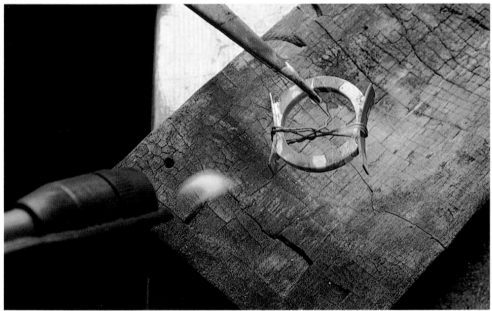

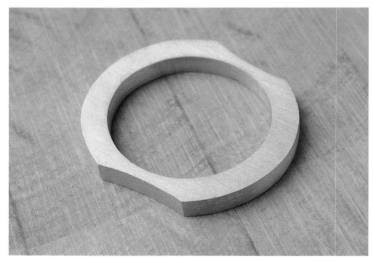

▲ 12. Apply heat. Since the solder needs to run along all four sides of the caps, it is best to use a gas soldering torch and solder paillons, rather than a water torch.

◄ 13. Once the ring is pickled, file and sand all the surfaces with emery paper, progressively increasing the grade of paper until the entire surface is smooth.

Construction of a Mounting from Simple Shapes

Knowing how to make and use different combinations of the elemental shapes is at the foundation of jewelry making. In a prior section we demonstrated how to make these shapes—sheet, wire, and tube—using fairly large pieces. Here we will show that even this tiny mounting is essentially made up of the same shapes.

Up to this point we have completed a hollow ring that is enclosed on all sides. If you apply heat to an enclosed hollow piece, the expansion of air inside will escape from the weakest point and cause it to crack. To avoid this make a tiny hole in the ring that will later be covered by a plaque with the designer's signature.

◄ 1. First, cut a V-shape out of the ring where the mounting will be placed. On the other side, make a small hole. Bend a sheet into a V-shape and solder it with hard gold solder.

▲ 2. Make a square wire and solder it to a small curved sheet. File, bend, and solder the square wire as shown so that it is capable of supporting a stone.

◄(center) 3. Next, join the wire unit to the V-shaped mount. Use hard paste solder for soldering and heat-shielding paste to support delicate pieces during the soldering process.

► 5. A gold wire is placed over the stone so that it will not fall out. The wire is secured by wetting it with flux at each end and applying the water torch rapidly and precisely; this will form a small ball at either end. Finish with a round rotary bur.

▲ 4. The mounting is complete. Next, fit it to the ring. Once the two elements, the mounting and the ring, are in their correct positions, tie them with steel wire so they are secure during soldering. Use a medium gold solder.

◄ And the final result. Work by Carles Codina

Filing and Sanding

Filing and sanding are two processes that are used constantly during the construction of a piece. They appear to be easily accomplished tasks but in fact they are two of the most difficult to master, and affect the final look of the piece.

Filing

Files usually come in three grades or teeth sizes. The larger the teeth, the more metal they are capable of cutting. At the same time, however, large teeth leave deeper cuts that are more time consuming to sand down later with *emery paper*.

Keep in mind that steel files only cut when stroked forward, so this is the stroke in which you want to apply pressure. Applying pressure when drawing the file backward only wears out the teeth. Diamond files are another type of file used in jewelry making. These cut much more uniformly and don't leave cuts as deep as the steel files do, making sanding less laborious.

The Care and Cleaning of Files

Files require special care to keep them in top condition. Keep them separate from other tools so that their teeth do not get dulled by contact with other surfaces. It's not a good idea to use quality files on soft metals such as copper because they become easily clogged with the metal. Designate files for use only with gold; keep them in separate cases.

Soft metals or contaminating metals such as lead leave small scraps of the metal that catch in the teeth, and can later damage or contaminate the piece you're working on.

To clean files, use a special file card or wash them well with gasoline. Never apply oil to a file, and avoid excessive heat if you decide to use flame to attach a handle.

◄ File cuts on the surface of a piece leave interesting results in the final finish. Work by Carles Codina

▲ Files come in many shapes, sizes, and cuts. This illustration shows the most common ones. Having a good set of files is essential in beginning the craft of jewelry making.

➤ To begin filing, you will need at least two different sizes of medium grade files of the various shapes (round, flat, triangular, square). Various small files of medium and fine grades will also be useful.

◄ To file a piece correctly, apply pressure as you push the file forward. One of the most frequent mistakes made by beginners is to inadvertently round off the edges; this comes from holding the file incorrectly. Concentration improves control of the file.

◄ A carpenter's square helps in the formation of a perfectly square sheet of metal with 90° corners. First file one side straight and place it in the square. Holding it up to the light, you can see where the edges of the sheet meet the carpenter's square. Continue filing at the points where there is the most contact with the square until the entire edge of the sheet lines up with the square. Do this to all four sides.

Grinding (Abrasives)

The following process eliminates the cuts produced by filing. For this we use various kinds of abrasive emery papers that are made of carborundum powder. As you sand, use progressively finer grades of emery paper.

If you have a grading system that goes from 150 to 1,200, you would only need three grades of paper—the first between 150 and 350, the second between 350 and 650, and the last between 1,000 and 1,200. A good proportion between grades would be, for example, to start with a grade of 350 to 400, then use one between 650 and 700, and finish with a fine grade of 1,000 or 1,200.

Progressing from one grade to the next eliminates the marks left by the grade you just used. Don't change grades until the previous marks are gone. Filing, then sanding, in a single direction will deepen, not eliminate, the marks. Instead, constantly crisscross the direction in which you sand. Use a very fine grade of emery paper (800–1200) for final sanding. The surface should be completely free of marks.

▲ For the best results, purchase a good quality emery paper. If you cut it well and take good care of it, it will last a long time. A variety of grading systems and qualities of emery paper is available, depending upon the manufacturer.

◄ To most precisely use emery paper with the least amount of waste, glue different grades of paper to various shapes of wooden sticks. While you can buy these ready-made, they are very simple tools to make yourself. The sticks will help you to better control the sanding, as well as to extend the life of the emery paper.

▲ Cut the emery paper to size and glue it to the stick with white carpenter's glue, making sure you line up the edge of the paper with a corner of the wooden stick. Before folding it, score the paper with a scissor point for accuracy.

▲ Change directions every time you change the grade of paper, and sand until the surface is left completely smooth.

▼ When you use an emery wheel, always wear protective goggles and a respirator, and use a dust collector cabinet to avoid the impact of flying metal particles, diminish their dispersion, and aid in their recovery.

▲ Another option is to use an emery wheel for sanding. Prepare a wheel by cutting a strip of emery paper approximately 1 cm in width, and fasten it to the end of the wheel bit with steel binding wire.

▲ An emery wheel is very useful for many other tasks, such as sanding ring interiors. Use caution, however, as it can leave marks, especially on flat surfaces.

Piercing

I f we had to select one tool that would best represent the craft of jewelry, it would without a doubt be a *jeweler's saw*. Its origin is ancient, dating as far back as the stone saws of the Neolithic Age. The ancient Romans developed a saw frame similar to the one we use today. Piercing and sawing cutouts are two closely linked processes, since it is impossible to cut out the interior of a metal sheet or piece without first piercing it.

➤ A preColumbian gold pectoral, belonging to the Tolima culture of Colombia, is a fine example of the jeweler's craft in its demonstration of piercing and cutout work, as well as the formal simplicity of design in this representation of the human form.

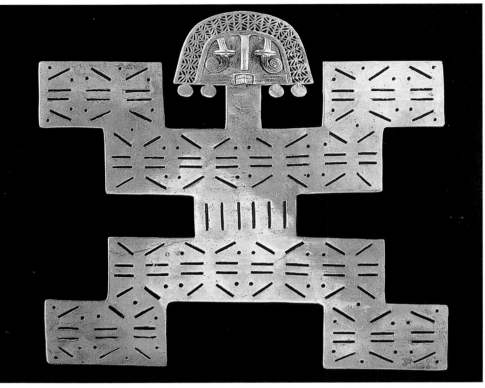

Cutting

Sawing holes and negative shapes consists of cutting and eliminating a small portion of material in the interior of a piece, either for decorative purposes, or to fit another material in its interior. A jeweler's saw can cut the majority of metals and materials used in the craft. It is made of two parts: an adjustable steel frame in the shape of an arc, and saw blades that are mounted within the frame at both ends. The *saw blade* is, naturally, the part that produces the cut. These blades are available in various sizes and are identified by the manufacturer's numbering systems. The selection of thickness depends upon the thickness of the metal to be cut.

▼ An example of cut elements of metal fastened together to form the final piece. Earrings designed by Stephane Landureau

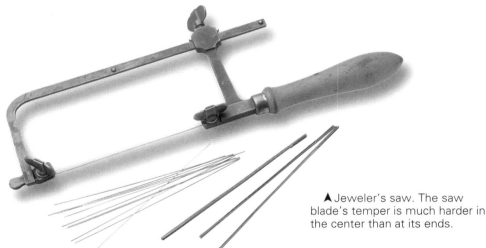

▲Jeweler's saw. The saw blade's temper is much harder in the center than at its ends.

➤ Negative shapes and holes are made by eliminating an interior part of a metal sheet. The metal is first pierced with a drill so that the saw blade can be inserted. Brooch by Aureli Bisbe

Sawing

The main function of a saw is, of course, to cut all the various types of metal and materials used in jewelry making. But it has other uses as well, such as filing inaccessible corners, or decorating a piece with small cuts on its surface.

Choose the size of the saw blade according to the thickness of the metal that will be cut. Never cut a thin sheet with a thick blade. If the distance between the teeth of the blade is larger than the sheet's thickness, the blade will most likely catch and break.

A lubricating wax applied to the blade eases the cutting action. Lubricating waxes for blades and other types of cutting tools are available commercially.

◄ To insert the blade in the saw frame, support the front end of the frame in the bench pin, and set the blade in the back clamp so that the teeth face toward you. With your shoulder, press gently against the frame, and set the other end of the blade in the front clamp; tighten the wing nut. When you release the pressure from the frame, the blade will be taut.

◄ The sawing movement should always be perpendicular to the piece, applying force on the downward movement. The saw cuts on the downward thrust due to the pitch of the saw blade's teeth.

◄ To transfer a paper drawing to a piece of metal, use carbon paper and china white.

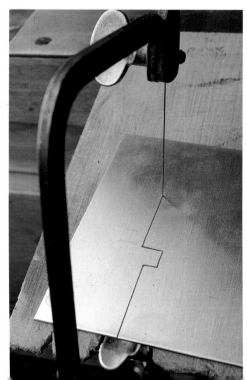

◄ To change the direction of sawing, pivot while sawing two or three times in place, to free the saw up a little. This way you can change direction easily without breaking the saw blade.

➤ To saw out an interior shape, first make a hole with a drill and insert the blade through it.

Transferring Drawings

A fast and easy method of transferring a drawing from paper to metal is to paint the surface of the metal with *china white*. Once the paint is dry, place carbon paper on the metal, and on top of this, the drawing you want to copy. Trace the drawing twice to transfer the carbon to the paint.

If the drawing transfers clearly, begin sawing by following the transfer lines on the paint. If not, go over the lines again with a scriber so that the drawing is lightly etched into the metal itself; then wash off the paint before sawing.

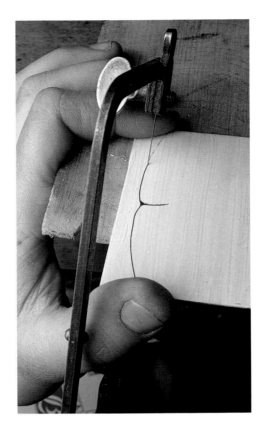
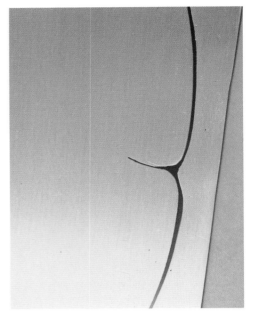

➤ Grasp the metal firmly and saw with long, firm vertical motions.

▲ In this example, the jeweler's saw not only served to cut the design, but also to file the inaccessible interior of the cut. This is done by applying light pressure with the side of the blade while sliding it up and down.

The Making of a Brooch by Aureli Bisbe

Occasionally, as we will see in this section, *cutouts* can be used to show off and give importance to other materials. Aureli Bisbe created a series of cutout box-like structures that, once mounted, frame and highlight a material that cannot be soldered—in this case, plastic countertop material.

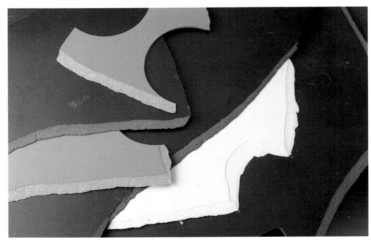

◄ The plastic countertop material is broken irregularly so as to enhance the texture at the break in the material. These pieces will be cut with a jeweler's saw and filed so they fit inside the metal frame.

◄ These are the structures which, once finished, will house the plastic.

➤ Brooches of plastic countertop material by Aureli Bisbe

Drilling and Grinding

Drilling and grinding are two different ways to cut and eliminate metal. Both are essential processes in jewelry making—especially in setting precious stones. Many times, drilling can also be used as a decorative element. These processes use *micro motors* and *flex shafts*, some of the most frequently used tools in a jeweler's workshop.

▲ Plastic ring, pierced with a bit, by Kepa Carmona

◄ Perforations in this brooch by Joaquim Capdevila give the piece an artistic quality.

Micro Motors and Flexible Shafts

Micro motor and flexible shaft machines are tools used for drilling and grinding. They have similar functions, but the results they give, and their versatility and ease of use, vary considerably. Micro motors have a small motor situated in the handpiece, while the flexible shaft's motor is separate from the handpiece; it transmits the drilling motion through a flexible arm or shaft.

Both instruments are essential in a workshop because they are also used to polish and set stones. The chuck of these drills, as well as the *bits* and *burs*, has a standard diameter of 2.35 mm, with a wide variety of interchangeable accessories. The difference between a bur and a bit is substantial. A bit can only cut vertically, whereas a bur is designed to cut laterally. Before beginning to drill, use a scriber to mark the hole's placement exactly. This point of reference helps prevent errors.

◄ These two types of cuts illustrate the different functions of bits and burs. While the bit simply makes a hole, the bur can take away metal in all directions.

➤ The flexible shaft is a tool used for drilling. It differs from a micro motor in that its motor connects to a flexible shaft, which transmits the motor's rotation to the handpiece.

▼ There are many different types of grinding burs, made of both steel and diamond. These are the most frequently used shapes.

Soldering

Soldering (from the Latin *solidare*, meaning "to make solid"), forms a solid, invisible union between separate metal elements in the construction of a piece. For thousands of years, a wide variety of techniques have been employed to join one piece of metal to another or to join metal to different kinds of materials, such as leather fasteners, rivets, and glue. In this section we discuss some of the types of cold connections that contemporary jewelers still incorporate today.

Soldering is the most commonly used technique for joining metal together, utilizing the interaction of the structure of the metals when heated. As we saw in the chapter on metallurgy, when metal is melted, its internal structure collapses, destroying the bond between the crystals, causing the metal to lose its original form. The same thing that happens in annealing also occurs in soldering—the groups of crystals separate and form microscopic spaces within the structure. Melted solder penetrates to the interior of the metal, creating a very strong union, known as a hard soldering.

◄ A master of soldering techniques can join various elements and create pieces, such as this gold bangle from Indonesia.

➤ Soldering is the basic process in the construction of many metal structures, such as this brooch by Ramón Puig Cuyàs.

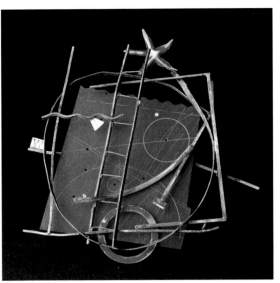

◄ Solder in the form of paillons and paste. Paste comes in a syringe so that it can be applied in measured amounts.

The Process

In the process of soldering, two basic elements interact: solder and heat. *Solder* is an alloy used to join metals that have higher melting points. The heat of a soldering *torch* causes solder to melt before the metals do. The melted solder flows on the surface of the join the same way the principle of capillarity works with water, filling the solder seam and connecting the separate elements of a piece.

You can make your own solder, but prepared solder is readily available. When soldering relatively complicated pieces of jewelry, you will have a minimum of three or four solders, each with a different melting point. Solders are sometimes numbered to indicate their melting points. Hard solders have higher melting points than medium and easy solders.

Solder comes in forms to suit a variety of applications. Two of the most common types are snippets, or *paillons*, cut from sheet or wire solder. Paste solder is becoming more popular to use because it doesn't require the use of soldering flux, and is especially good to use with a water torch.

Gas Torches

Solder can be found in any specialty store, but knowing which solder to use for which metal is more complicated. It's also important to know something about the equipment and accessories used in soldering.

Soldering Blocks and Platforms

There are many types of blocks and other platforms that can withstand the heat of the soldering torch: ceramic fiber blocks, wire frames, various types of rotating platforms, and blocks of soft refractory material, such as magnesia, that facilitate precision work.

Wire frames allow for even distribution of heat on piece. This kind of platform is perfect for making joins in which the solder needs to flow over the whole piece. A charcoal block is also useful because it doesn't create as much oxidation on the piece, and it distributes and maintains its own even heat. Many of the exercises in this book are done on this type of block.

◄ Use a block or pad when applying heat to a piece.

Soldering Flux

The use of soldering flux is very important, because soldering causes surface oxidation that prevents the solder from flowing evenly.

The most common flux is a mix of borax and water. Boric acid can be added to the mixture to raise the melting point. Borax has one drawback—when heated, it bubbles slightly, causing the paillons to move out of position. Borax should be applied with a brush to both sides of the piece after it has been cleaned of oxide.

▼ Liquid flux and a bar of powdered borax; when dissolved in water, they aid the flow of solder, especially when used with silver.

▼ Antioxidant chemicals, or commercial products applied before soldering, form a film that prevents oxidation and protects the finish from the heat.

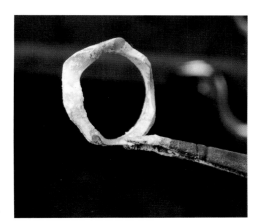

Gas Torches

Torches are used to heat the metal so that the nearby solder will reach its melting point by indirect heat, and join the pieces together. Torches are used for annealing, too. The torches used in jewelry making usually contain some type of gas, plus air pressure produced by a *foot* or *hand bellows*, a motor-driven *compressor*, or even a *blowpipe*.

The propane canister torch is commonly used in small workshops. Air is fed with a foot bellows or a small electric air compressor. There are also models that generate enough pressure from the cylinder to eliminate the need for additional air. These soldering torches are more precise, but they are not as adjustable.

A water torch is very useful in jewelry making because it directs heat only in the desired area. However, fewer types of solder can be used with it. This torch allows you to solder more rapidly, more precisely, and with less oxidation. It is not very useful when used directly on paillons, because the force of the flame causes the paillons to move out of place. However, you can quickly get good results with paste solder because flux does not need to be applied.

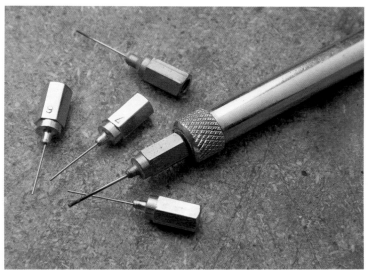

▲ The flame of the water torch, with its characteristic green color, is capable of reaching a temperature of more than 3,000°C. The powerful, precise flame can be used to solder pieces with speed and accuracy.

▲ ▼ Regulating the quantity of air and gas mixed by the soldering torch controls the flame's intensity. Use a reducing flame for annealing and uniform soldering, or an oxidizing flame for greater intensity and precision, although the latter creates more oxidation.

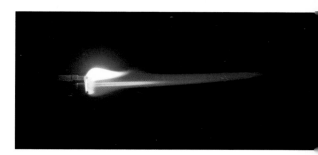

◄ A very useful type of soldering torch is the water torch. It breaks down distilled water into oxygen and hydrogen. The intensity of the flame is regulated by changing the tips.

Application

Before soldering, remove any oxide and oils from the metal by pickling it in acid or another pickling solution. Then rinse well with water and sodium bicarbonate to remove the acid.

To create a solid solder seam, make sure you don't use too much solder. Less solder is needed when the pieces fit together as closely as possible. Soldering correctly requires a little practice, and there are a few essentials to remember. Melted solder is attracted by heat and always flows toward the hottest point, so it's very important to heat the entire piece gently and evenly. If you heat the solder without heating the piece first, it melts and forms a ball that cannot penetrate the join. By the same token, the two pieces you want to connect must be heated equally. If one side is hotter than the other, the solder will fuse more strongly to it.

Normally, jewelers work with three types of solder, each having a different melting point, which are classified and used accordingly. For the first soldering of a piece, use hard solder that has the highest melting point. Then, when applying solder for the second time, use one with a lower melting point so that the first will not remelt.

▼ 3. Heat the entire piece until it turns a dark color, then concentrate the torch on the join until the join turns a cherry red. This is the moment when the solder begins to flow. It will be visible as a bright line. Finally, reduce or turn off the flame. When cooled, the solder will have created a sound join.

▲ A perfect join depends upon a perfect fit. In this case, the seam will not be very strong since the two sides don't fit together well.

▼ 1. First apply the flux and then, with the same brush or a pair of tweezers, place the paillon of solder on the join. Warm the piece slightly after applying the flux so that the paillon stays in place. To use paste solder also warm the piece slightly before applying it. When it penetrates the interior, apply more heat. When using wire solder, wet the wire with flux first.

▲ Now the cut in the ring is a clean one. As soon as it has been adjusted to fit closer together and fastened with binding wire, it will be ready to solder.

▲ 2. Space just enough solder paillons necessary for the join you're making. Excess solder is difficult to remove from complex shapes, such as those shown here.

➤ When soldering delicate pieces, the different elements often move. To prevent movement, tie them together with binding wire. You can purchase this wire in different thicknesses. Remove the wire before pickling.

◄ Commercial heat-shielding paste holds elements in position while soldering. It is also used to protect gems from heat, especially when repairing jewelry with gemstones.

➤ You can also protect solder by using yellow ochre dissolved in water, or you can buy products made for this purpose. To avoid letting gemstones come into contact with heat, use the heat-shielding paste.

Hollow Construction

Dimension may be created by *chasing* (see page 88) or *dapping* (see page 50), and also by joining different shapes of wire onto sheets.

➤ This type of construction requires a rectangular-shaped backing which you later remove by cutting a series of bevels around the dimensional shape. Bend and break off the excess metal with a pair of small pliers.

➤ Once the piece is soldered, file and sand the entire exterior shape until the structure is smooth.

Safety

All soldering torches use some kind of gas. Your equipment supplier should sell only authorized soldering torches with their correct hoses. These hoses should be changed when they become worn or are defective. It's also important that your torch has filters, flashback arrestors, valves, and other safety features. Don't forget that the workspace must have adequate ventilation for the type of gas being used. Never use soldering blocks containing asbestos. Asbestos is a toxic material and its use is ill-advised.

➤ A piece constructed from different shapes made of rectangular silver wire and sheet copper. Work by Xavier Ines

Eliminating Oxides

Once the piece has cooled, remove the surface *oxide* with a pickling solution before continuing work. In the chapter on metallurgy, different ways to eliminate oxide were discussed. It's worth reiterating here that you can minimize this oxidation by using appropriate antioxidants, and after pickling a piece in acid, rinse it thoroughly in water with a little baking soda. After the piece is clean, dry it well so as not to rust your files and other tools, especially the rolling mill.

Used Acid

Old or used pickling acid can be saved and used as a copper-plating solution, because the acid becomes saturated with an excess of free ions. Putting metal in the acid creates an electric charge that makes the ions adhere to the surface. You can see this process clearly when you drop a piece of binding wire or steel tweezers in the acid. Any ferrous metal creates an exchange of electric ions.

The effect caused by the used acid is very interesting when used to charge copper in the process of granulation or gold or silver plating.

Neutralize saturated acid with baking soda or calcium carbonate before discarding.

Other Types of Joins

Soldering has been and will continue to be the most frequently used technique for joining elements in the construction of metal objects. The evolution of contemporary jewelry, however, has brought about the extensive use of materials which cannot be soldered, and requires joins that do not affect the form and expressive quality of the material. A wide variety of innovative types of joins is commonly found in contemporary works of jewelry.

> ➤ The use of plastic adhesives is growing more popular due to the use of dissimilar materials in jewelry making. Brooch by Carles Codina

Screws

Screws, as well as rivets, enable us to make cold connections between various materials, such as plastic and wood. The use of screws has become increasingly popular because it is a very precise and clean process.

To make screws you'll need a set of *hand taps* and their corresponding *circular dies*. These steel tools are designed to cut softer, less durable metals.

▲ Brooch of different materials assembled with screws. Work by Kepa Carmona

◄ 1. For this example, anneal and draw a silver wire to the appropriate diameter for the construction of your piece. Next, insert the wire into a circular die of the same diameter, which is held securely by a die holder. Turning the die holder in a clockwise direction produces the exterior cut of screw threads on the wire.

◄ 2. Construct the female counterpart from a silver tube whose interior diameter is slightly smaller than the exterior diameter of the wire. Normally, hand taps come in sets of three, with different cutting functions to be used in a particular order. Turning them in a tap wrench cuts the threads on the inside of the tube.

◄ 3. The size of the threaded wire and its female counterpart must have the same pitch, which is the distance between the teeth of the thread, in order to fit together correctly.

▼ A screwdriver fits easily into a saw cut on the top of a gold wire. Brooch by Carles Codina

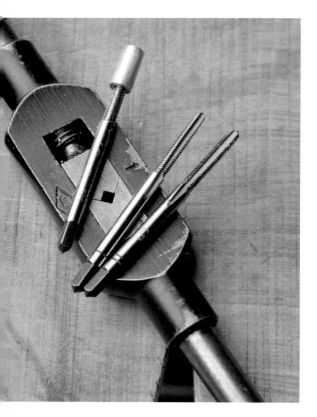

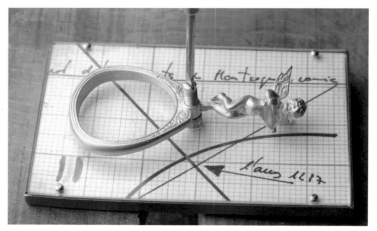

Rivets

Rivets are not new. Their origins are more ancient than those of soldering and are based on the principles of malleability and deformation of cold metal. The process consists of forcing an annealed piece, usually a wire, into a tight space or hole until the wire's shape conforms to that of the hole so it can't fall out or be easily removed.

➤ 1. To make a rivet, wet the end of a round wire with soldering flux. Hold it vertically upside down with tweezers and apply intense heat until the wire melts and forms a small ball at its end.

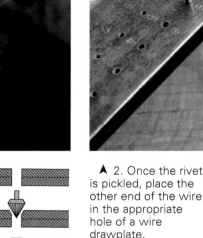

▲ 2. Once the rivet is pickled, place the other end of the wire in the appropriate hole of a wire drawplate.

▲ 3. Strike the wire with a jeweler's hammer until the head is flat.

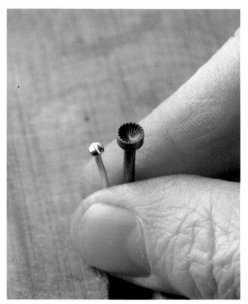

▲ 4. With a file and/or a concave bur, put the desired finish on the head of the rivet.

➤ One approach is to rivet only one side of a piece, leaving the other side decorative.

Diagram of the riveting process

Adhesives

Much of the construction of jewelry today would not be possible without adhesives. There are many good quality adhesives available, capable of very powerful bonding.

Out of the wide range of adhesives that exist on the market, select the one most appropriate for the type of join you want and the material you are using. The join should never be stronger than the material. Create a slightly rough surface by filing or sanding both points of contact and then clean the surface thoroughly before gluing.

Two-part epoxies are more appropriate for joins that need to be filled, or for pieces that will be subject to light vibrations or movements. These adhesives are also good to use on porous materials; unlike *cyanoacrylate glues*, they do not become stiff, and therefore do a better job of joining smooth surfaces of different materials.

Brooch by Aureli Bisbe

The artist soldered two concentric arcs of rectangular silver wire onto a silver sheet, then used a bur to grind away successive layers of heat-resistant, chemical-resistant plastic, layered to appear as though they were laminated.

➤ 1. Cut circular rings out of different shades of the plastic so that they fit inside the silver brooch. Use a compass to mark the correct size before cutting.

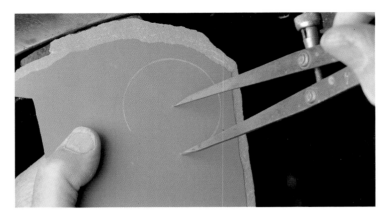

◄ 2. Next, use a saw to cut just outside the compass mark, and smooth off the edges with a file so that the concentric material is perfectly shaped.

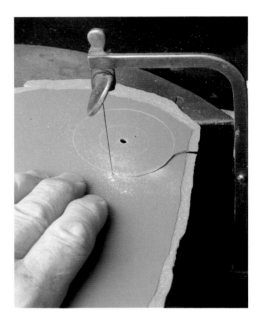

➤ 3. Make sure the three layers of plastic fit perfectly inside the silver piece. Once adjusted to fit, glue in place.

▼ 4. Apply a layer of epoxy to a clean surface, free of oils, and insert the first ring.

▼ 5. Without waiting for the first ring to dry, apply more adhesive and place the second ring atop the first.

▼ 6. Repeat this process for the final ring.

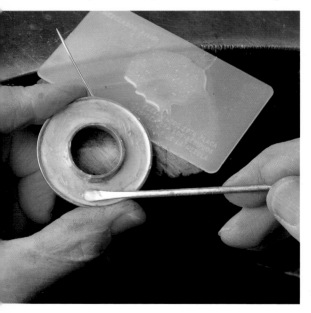

▲ 7. Place the piece firmly between three clamps so that the pressure makes the layer of adhesive as thin as possible. You can speed up the drying process by placing a high-wattage light bulb underneath.

➤ 9. Keep cutting toward the interior, supporting the piece on your bench pin.

▲ 8. Once dry, mill the material away with a round bur, starting from the exterior edge of the piece and working toward the center, so that the successive layers begin to appear from underneath.

▲ 10. Work the silver border of the piece with the same bur, exactly like the plastic.

➤ This is the result after milling all of the plastic disks. Brooches by Aureli Bisbe

Making Domes and Cylinders

The great majority of jewelry pieces begin from the basic form of a sheet or a wire. Chasing and dapping create dimension on a flat surface. But many times a three-dimensional form is needed for hiding a closure, constructing a sphere, or curving a plane.

➤ The basic tools needed to shape domes and cylinders are dapping blocks, which can be made of bronze or steel; a grooved forming block on which one can form cylinders; and dapping punches that can perform different functions.

Making a Dome

To construct elements such as clasps, spheres, or caps, start by cutting and shaping a disk into a hemisphere; disks used by themselves as purely formal elements can also produce interesting effects.

It's important to know how much metal, in grams, is needed to make a dome, especially if you are making the piece from gold. This formula uses the specific gravity of the metal. The specific gravity of gold is 15.5.

$$\frac{Radius^2 \times 3.14 \times Thickness \times Specific\ Gravity}{1,000} = Weight\ of\ disk\ in\ grams$$

For example, how much would a 1-millimeter-thick disk of gold weigh if it had a diameter of 14 mm?

$$\frac{(7 \times 7) \times 3.14 \times 1 \times 15.5}{1,000} = 2.3\ g\ of\ gold$$

The kind of dapping (or doming) *punches* and blocks used to shape a disk is very important. When steel punches and blocks are used to shape a disk of gold or silver, the disk will become thinner as it is struck. For this reason, it is better to use punches and blocks made of wood which will not affect the thickness as much as one made of steel. The way in which you strike the disk is also very important. The dapping punch should move slightly as you strike it with a mallet, as if it were a burnisher. Avoid sharp blows that could slip on the surface of the metal. This will help to form a dome of uniform thickness.

➤ 4. The metal hardens during the process of shaping the dome. Control this by annealing the disk regularly.

▼ Necklace made from two sheets shaped in silver. Work by Xavier Doménech

◄ Once a disk is marked on a sheet with a compass it can be cut with a jeweler's saw, but the more appropriate tool made for this purpose is the disc cutter, which has circular cutting plates and punches that come in various diameters.

▲ 1. Insert a sheet of annealed metal into a disk cutter and strike the punch crisply and concisely with a hammer to cut a disk of the desired size.

▲ 2. To shape the disk into a hemisphere, place it in the first cup of the dapping block in which it fits level, just below the surface. Begin striking the disk with a punch that is slightly larger than the cup you are using.

▲ 3. To continue shaping the dome, progressively reduce the diameter of the cup and punch until you reach the diameter needed. In order to form a perfect hemisphere, the dome should turn slightly as you strike it on its interior surface.

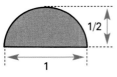

▲ Measure the dome with a gauge to be sure it is perfectly hemispherical. When its height is half its diameter, it is a perfect hemisphere and can be joined to another hemisphere to make a round ball.

➤ Necklace made from disks of oxidized silver and paper. Work by Ana Pavicevik

◄ Detail of necklace

Making a Cylinder

The cylinder is another much-used form in the joining of separate elements. It is shaped by placing the metal on a grooved forming block, with the shank of a dapping punch placed on top and striking the shank with a mallet.

➤ 1. To prepare a cylinder, cut and anneal a rectangular sheet of metal. Begin shaping the metal in a grooved forming block, taking care that the edges of the channel don't mar the sheet, because the damage is very difficult to repair.

▲ 2. Keep reducing the diameter of the dapping shank and the size of the channel little by little. When the sheet is in the form of a "U", strike it on the exterior until the edges of the sheet come together.

▲ 3. Before soldering, tie the cylinder with binding wire to keep it from opening in the heat due to the tension created by the shaping process.

➤ 4. Once the cylinder is pickled in nitric acid, place a punch in the interior and strike it lightly with a plastic mallet on the exterior to put the final touches on the form. When it is finished, sand it with emery paper.

Making a Clasp

Next, we will see how the two shapes treated in this section can by applied to make a cap for the clasp of a necklace. The necklace is also shown in the chapter Step by Step (page 150).

➤ 1. Prepare two domes and two small cylinders, as previously described, so that their exterior diameters are of the same size and can be fit together.

➤ 2. Apply solder to join the dome and cylinder pieces together.

◄ 3. After filing and sanding the unit, solder a thick ring to the top of the cylinder; then make a transversal hole through which you will insert a gold wire, so that it passes through the braid of the necklace and comes out the other side. Next, solder the two ends of the wire to the cap and remove the excess wire.

➤ 4. This is the closure after polishing. Here we have attached a clasp that is available from a supplier of jewelry findings.

Forging

One of the most ancient forms of working with metal known to humankind is forging—working metal with different hammers on *anvils*, *stakes*, and *surface plates,* to affect its shape and size. The technique of forging allows for the formation of shapes with bulk and weight, as well as those of delicate detail, and creates harmonious transitions between thick and thin shapes within a piece.

As with rolling, the process of forging also work-hardens the internal structure of the metal. When worked, the size of the crystals creates a more durable metal than that of melted metal. For this reason, repeated hammering allows you to obtain very strong but delicate-looking textured surfaces.

Forging essentially consists of shaping metal with force, working it with hammers that are usually squared and flat at one end and wedge-shaped on the other. When one strikes a metal rod using the wedge-shaped end of the hammer, the metal is forced out lengthwise upon the axis of the wedge, causing the metal to stretch in that direction.

To widen an ingot, rod, or another metal shape, use the flat side of the hammer and strike it upon the full surface of the metal so that it expands outward.

Metal is forged using anvils or different shaped steel blocks called stakes—the shape and size used depends upon the nature of the piece being worked. It's important that the surface of the steel be stable and as smooth as possible. In the same way, the hammer should be well polished, since with every strike it transfers its finish onto that of the metal.

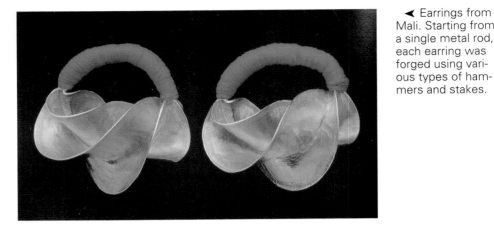

◄ Earrings from Mali. Starting from a single metal rod, each earring was forged using various types of hammers and stakes.

Gold, silver and copper are all suitable metals for forging since they are among the softest and most malleable, but brass is not.

As you progress in the forging of a piece, the metal will become harder and therefore must be regularly annealed. Review the chapter on metallurgy (see pages 12–25) to familiarize yourself again with the specifics of annealing and cooling the various alloys, and the points at which they reach sufficient malleability.

▲ Silver pendant made from repeated elongations of the metal. Work by Jaime Díaz

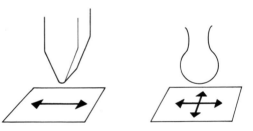

◄ Striking the metal with the cross peen end of the hammer produces a lengthwise enlargement of the rod, while hitting with the slightly domed end creates an extension in all directions.

◄ The kind of hammer used and the way the metal is struck are factors that determine the outcome of the forged piece.

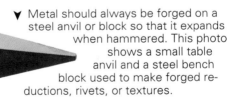

▼ Metal should always be forged on a steel anvil or block so that it expands when hammered. This photo shows a small table anvil and a steel bench block used to make forged reductions, rivets, or textures.

Forged Bracelet

For the following bracelet, Jaime Díaz used a silver ingot and forged it with a hammer and a plastic mallet using various steel stakes.

➤ 1. Start with an 3.5 mm ingot weighing 80 grams.

▲ 2. Hammer the ingot on a small stake. This one was especially modified from an old hammer for the purpose of creating this concave shape.

▲ 3. Place the bracelet on a slightly curved, larger stake adapted from a machine part. Strike it on the exterior, enlarging the outside diameter and texturing the surface.

▲ 4. After annealing to a minimum of 750°C and cooling it abruptly in water, the bracelet is ready to be hammered again.

▲ 5. Put the piece on a bracelet mandrel and hammer it with a mallet of nylon or wood to shape the oval interior more precisely.

◄ 6. Return to the original stake and hammer on the exterior, to finish the edges and improve the texture.

➤ 7. Make two identical pieces and then solder them together. The interior is left oxidized while the exterior is rubbed lightly with fine steel wool, taking care not to damage the hammered texture.

Hinges and Hinge Structures

Many jewelry pieces, especially necklaces and bracelets, are made of smaller parts that need to be hinged or linked together to allow for movement and to adapt to the shape of the body. There are many possible variations of the hinges and hinge structures shown in this book; we will demonstrate how to make three of the most common and most useful ones: a wire hinge, a tube hinge, and a blind hinge.

◄ Painted plastic bracelets made of interlocking, multi dimensional shapes. The design of the links, and the movement they allow, lend interest and charm to the piece.

Wire Hinge

There are many variations of this hinge and they can be used in a variety of ways. Normally they are used to link tennis bracelet settings together, as well as other types of elements. One of these variations is the linked bracelet that appears in the chapter Step by Step.

To make the following pendant, first prepare a rectangular wire and use it to make a series of rings of different diameters. Solder and sand the rings.

▲ 1. Drill two holes on the side of one ring. The holes should be separated from one another by no more than 1.5 mm.

▲ 2. In a second ring, drill two more holes exactly like those of the first ring. Remove the metal between the two holes with a cylindrical bur. Next, with a thinner cylindrical bur than the first, grind a vertical channel between the two holes. Fit a small wire in this channel and solder it into place.

▼ 3. Shape a .6 mm round wire into a "U" and insert it into the second ring. Then, insert the two ends of the wire into the two holes of the first ring, soldering the ends in place on the interior.

▲ 4. To ensure that there is sufficient movement in a grouping of such hinges, extend the U-shaped wires well past the holes in the second ring and solder only one side of each linkage to begin with. Next, hold the piece up so that the rings fall naturally, and solder the second side in place, to establish how much movement is needed when it is worn.

After soldering, pickle the grouping and cut off the excess wire, then file them smooth.

▼ 5. Make another small hole in each ring. Insert an annealed gold wire into the hole and use it to secure a river pearl and piece of coral to each of the rings.

Tube Hinge

Tube hinges are used frequently to allow movement in bracelets, boxes, and other elements of construction. They are very flexible, and can be made to fit various purposes and sizes.

For the next example, make a round tube from a .5 mm sheet and two squares from 2.5 mm square wire soldered with hard solder.

➤ 3. Solder the tube to one of the squares, using steel soldering pins as supports, making sure the bridge stays free of solder. Use medium solder.

▼ 5. Prepare an annealed wire that fits into the interior of the tube, and cut it to a length so that .5mm extends from the tube at either end. Rivet the wire to join the two pieces.

◄ 1. First fit the tube between the two square pieces. To do this, glue them onto a sheet and, with a round file, file the two edges of the squares until the tube fits snugly between them.

▲ 2. In one tube, cut a bridge with a jeweler's saw, as shown in the photo. The bridge serves as a spacer so that the two ends are perfectly aligned when soldered.

▲ 4. Once soldered, cut out the bridge, and cut another piece of tubing that fits snugly in the space left by the bridge. Solder this tube to the second square so that the squares are aligned when the tube is fit into place.

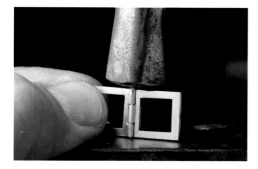

▲ Gold bracelet with tube hinges. Work by Carles Codina

Blind Hinge

This kind of hinge is traditionally used for rigid bracelets and other pieces in which it is important that the hinge be concealed.

To make a blind hinge, measure the piece and the size of the hinge very carefully before beginning. The first step is to shape the location on the piece where the hinge will be placed, so that the hinge fits very tightly.

This ring will be hinged in the middle in order to access a secret compartment. Long ago these compartments were used to conceal poisons.

▲ 1. Make a cut in the ring with a jeweler's saw. Next, widen this space using files and finally a cylindrical bur, such as that shown in the photo.

▲ 2.Make two tubes so that one fits perfectly inside the other. Make the outer tube substantially thicker so that it can be filed down later.

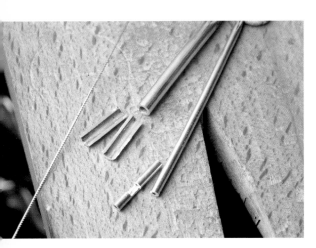

▲ 3. Cut the larger tube lengthwise down the middle. In the smaller one, cut a fitting in the form of a bridge, such as shown in the picture. This bridge serves as a spacer that will be removed later.

▲ 4. Using a medium solder, solder the small tube inside one of the larger halves so that the bridge remains exposed. Once soldered in place, cut the bridge out, leaving the two ends encased in the half-tube. To finish this part of the hinge, solder a piece of small tubing into the second half of the larger half-tubing so that it fits perfectly into the space left by the bridge in the first half.

▲ 5. The two tube pieces fit together well, and the outermost part fits perfectly into the space that was made for it in the ring. Cover the interior of the hinge with a solder inhibitor. You should also protect the delicate soldered points of the ring itself.

➤ 6. Once the hinge is in place, secure the ring with soft binding wire, and solder the hinge to the ring with soft solder.

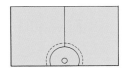

▲ Side view of a blind hinge

➤ 7. After cleaning and pickling, file down the outer tube of the hinge so that it is level with the contour of the ring. Be careful not to file through the small tube or the hinge will break.

➤ 8. Insert a round, annealed wire inside the small tube and rivet it on an anvil, so that striking it with a hammer on one end will cause the wire to rivet on both ends, simultaneously.

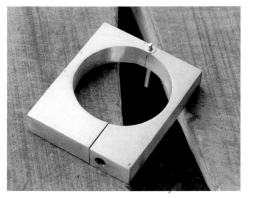

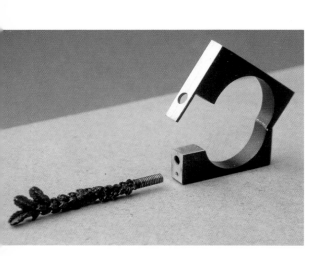

◄ 9. Saw through the ring on the side opposite the hinge, and solder the resulting openings closed with silver sheet to create two independent chambers capable of holding powder or liquid. The final touch is a cactus-shaped element that serves a specific purpose—one end is threaded to serve as a lid or stopper for the right chamber.

➤ *Ring for Dying. Protected Species No. 3* by Carles Codina

Closures (Clasps and Latches)

J ewelry is made to be displayed on the human body and to be admired by others. Pieces often require some sort of secure fastening mechanism. The form itself may serve to hold it in place, but most pieces—whether a bracelet, necklace, brooch, or some other kind of jewelry—need a closure.

Today, you can purchase all types of prefabricated clasps from jewelry-supply stores and catalogs. These closures are soldered or mounted so easily to different jewelry parts that in many cases it's only necessary to fit them properly and give

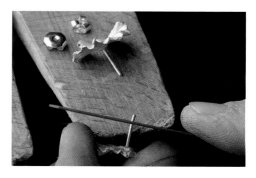

▲ Necklace with a closure adapted to the characteristics of the piece

them a final finish. However, sometimes a prefabricated clasp might interfere with a design. It is recommended that you know how these mechanisms function so that you can accurately adapt a clasp to the particular characteristics of a given piece.

▼ Different types of clasps can be purchased from jewelry supply stores.

Omega Clip

Perhaps one of the best earring closures is the *omega clip*, named for its shape. Its form allows for the best placement of an earring. The clip consists of a post that passes through the wearer's earlobe and another wire that presses the earlobe against the earring.

➤ The omega wire provides a functional tension and for this reason it should never be annealed. Keep this in mind for the purposes of repair as well: always remove the omega wire before soldering a broken piece. To rivet the wire in place, insert a small annealed wire through the support and the omega wire, and strike it with a hammer. Here a hammer handpiece is used together with a steel block to set the rivet.

◀ To make an earring back, the omega wire is mounted and a post is soldered approximately 7 to 9 mm from the support. First solder the support, then the post. After soldering, mount the omega.

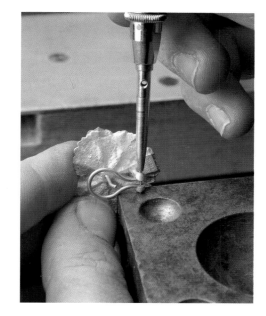

Friction Nuts
(Butterflys)

The base piece of this earring back consists of a silver or gold post about .7 mm thick, which should be firmly soldered to the piece as shown in the drawing. The nut itself can be purchased ready-made, but if you fabricate it yourself, don't forget that the metal for this type of nut should be under tension and therefore cannot be made from annealed metal.

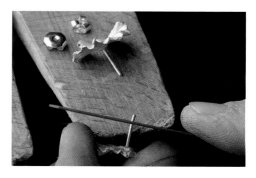

◀ Solder an earring post securely by making a small hole with a bur, then solder the post inside the hole.

◀ With the edge of a file, notch the post to hold the friction nut in place.

◀ This is the type of notch to use with a friction nut.

▼ Friction nuts can be purchased ready-made. You only need to select the size that fits the post.

Pin Back (Brooch Pin)

This very secure type of fastener can be adapted to any flat surface. It can be made in many ways; here is an easy method done in gold.

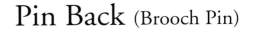

➤ 1. Make a tube of gold with a sheet .5 mm thick. On another sheet of the same thickness, cut a 90° groove using a square or triangular file.

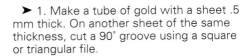

▲ 2. Bend the sheet at the groove and solder it into place, then attach the tube as shown. Now make a rectangular wire and similarly bevel, bend, and solder it as shown in the photo.

▲ 3. To make a good fit for the wire that will be inserted in the tube, first use an inverted cone bur to grind out the interior of the tube from both sides, as seen in the photo.

▲ 4. A second grinding with a cylindrical bur is necessary to make a small base for the wire to rest on.

▲ 5. When these two elements are finished, align and solder them parallel to each other with as much space between them as possible.

➤ 6. Insert an unannealed gold wire and bend it as shown in the photo.

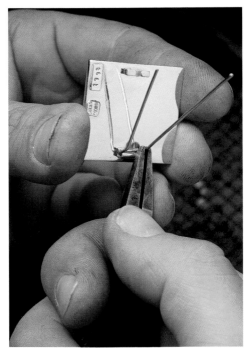

▼ 7. Align the wire so that the ends stay open and, when inserted into the closure, they exert an outward force on the closure's interior surface.

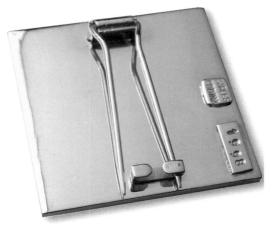

Box Clasp

The box clasp has many variations based on a structure like the one shown here. The bracelet project in this book (page 144) demonstrates in detail the simple adaptation of a box clasp.

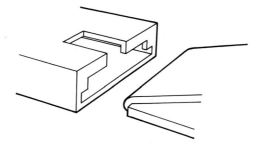

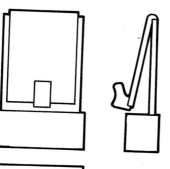

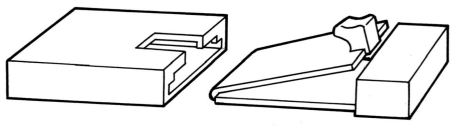

◄ The construction of a box clasp

Half-hinge Pin Catch for a Bracelet

Generally, this catch is used on bracelets. It is easy to make and allows room for many variations. Make a tube and cut it in three pieces. Solder two of these pieces to one end of the bracelet and the central part to the other. Through the center of the tubes runs a pin made of a bent half-round wire. Solder a small wire that spans the interior of one end of the catch to prevent the pin from falling out and getting lost. The pin can then be slid out, freeing the middle tube so the bracelet can open.

◄ A mounted tube clasp for a bracelet

Screw Clasp

As you read in the section on joins, it is easy to make a screw with the proper tools. In this case, adapting a screw to make a clasp is simple and can be done in a variety of ways.

◄ A screw clasp adaptation

Hook-and-Eye Clasp

This clasp is usually used to fasten necklaces and bracelets. The thickness and the temper of the wire are important factors, since a very fine annealed wire cannot withstand a great deal of use or any heavy weight.

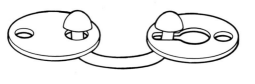

◄ Some options for making hook-and-eye clasps

Jump Rings

Jump rings are essential elements in jewelry making. They are used as movable links between separate parts and for making chains. Wrap lengths of metal wire around a jump ring mandrel into a tight spiral, then saw the rings, and either join them to one another or to the body of a piece.

Jump rings come in many shapes, but in this section we will focus on the simple and useful round jump ring. It is used to make the bracelet described here, but its uses are many. Be sure you have a mandrel of the desired size.

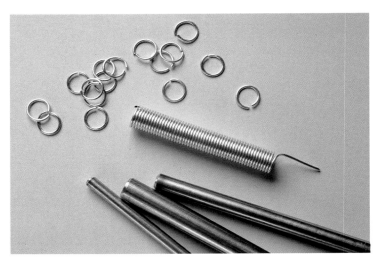

◄ Although there are specific tools on the market for making and cutting jump rings, the method described here is easy and economical. All you need is a hand drill and jump ring mandrels of various diameters.

▲1. First, mount the mandrel within a hand drill and fasten the drill handle firmly in a vise. Next, insert one end of the wire between the collet and the mandrel so that the end is secure. Then, putting a little tension on the wire, turn the drill handle slowly and smoothly. You can wind the wire directly onto the mandrel, or first cover the mandrel with a protective piece of paper.

➤ 2. The wrapping of the spiral has put them under tension. Anneal the spiral so the rings won't open during soldering, otherwise they will open slightly when soldered and the solder joints will not be strong. After the spiral is annealed, cut the rings with a jeweler's saw. Don't use bench scissors (jeweler's shears) because they create a gap in the rings that is too large to be securely soldered.

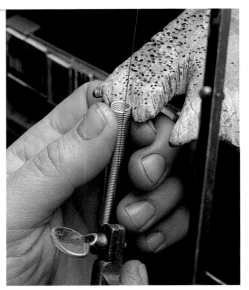

➤ Necklace made of different-sized jump rings. Work by Sofie Lambaert

Bracelet of Jump Rings

The construction of this bracelet is very simple, but one of surprising beauty, primarily due to its rather unorthodox matte finish. The closure, called a toggle clasp, is also very simple to make. Use annealed gold wire .7 mm thick and medium solder.

◄ Chains made of jump rings have been used since antiquity by many cultures, such as this Berber ornament from Tunisia.

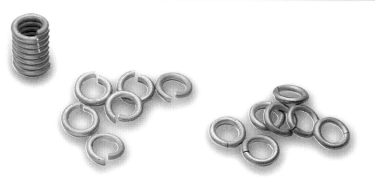

1. Make the coil on the mandrel. Anneal and pickle the coil, and then cut and close the rings using two flat-nosed pliers.

2. Place the rings on a charcoal brick for soldering. Heat them slightly before applying the torch so that the paste solder will thoroughly penetrate the metal.

3. Once soldered and pickled, forge the rings with a jeweler's or ball-peen hammer. Then cut half of the rings along the solder joint with a jeweler's saw.

4. Construct the bracelet by placing two closed rings inside an open one. Solder the open ring to form groups of three. Then join these groups together using another open ring, forming groups of seven.

5. Continue joining and soldering the rings until you have made a chain about 18 cm long—the average length of a bracelet.

6. The toggle clasp is easy to make. Solder the last ring of one end of the bracelet so that it cannot move. Now make a small chain of round rings soldered to a small rectangular bar, and solder this unit to the other end of the bracelet. The bar should just fit through the last ring of the bracelet for a secure closure.

7. The result is a classic chain, but the forging and etching with acid give it a different look.

Surfaces

Once you are familiar with the wide variety of preparation and execution of jewelry finishing techniques, take full advantage of the surface treatments presented in this chapter.

The following sections describe many different surface treatments for metal. Some techniques require prior preparation of different alloys to obtain color while others show how to create interesting surface textures and finishes.

Etching with Acid

Etching with acid has many uses in jewelry making, for example, in the application of niello, enamel, resin, and gem setting. It offers a wide range of application—anything from very detailed designs to large areas of interesting texture. Acid etching captures the subtle qualities of drawing so that designs made on paper can be transferred to the metal's surface easily and accurately.

The principle is simple. Acids that dissolve metal are called *mordants*. They are used together with resists of lacquer and varnish, so that the acid cannot dissolve the metal wherever the resist is applied. The combination of these two elements, acid and resists, produces wonderful effects.

Preparing the Metal

First, sand the metal and rub with pumice stone powder or with a fiberglass brush and water. Then clean and dry the piece well before applying the varnish. It is important that the metal is well-dried, or the varnish will not resist the acid properly.

Transferring the Design

There are a variety of ways to transfer a drawing to metal. Choose the method best suited to the design.

One way to transfer a detailed drawing is to paint the surface of the metal with white transfer paint so that it is completely covered. Place a sheet of carbon paper on top of the paint and then trace the drawing on top of the carbon paper. With a steel scribe or *graver* retrace the lines of the drawing in order to completely remove the paint from the design area.

▼ This brooch by Judith McCraig, entitled *The Outlook*, was etched in acid and later chased.

Resist Products

Choose the resist based on its ability to produce a particular effect. Glues, waxes, adhesive tapes, and mixtures of tar are all capable of interesting—and even surprising—results.

Hot beeswax and red flake shellac make good resists, though the latter is not as precise. For delicate work, use black satin varnish sold in art supply stores. This is a soft varnish that lends itself to tracing curves and complex designs, and it does not come off as easily as bitumen of Judea (*asphaltum*). To remove the wax, simply put the surface of the metal in boiling water and then wash with water and detergent. Always apply the resist in a fine, even coat and let it dry before tracing the design.

▲ Hot wax can be applied with a paintbrush or used in a wax melting pot.

▲ When using a wax melting pot, heat the metal slightly before putting it in the pot, to make sure the layer is not too thick.

▲ This surface is ready to be etched with a steel scriber or burin.

➤ Metal should be free of oils before etching. Handle by the edges only, because oils from the skin can affect the resist. Here, packing tape on the back of the piece extends beyond the edges so that it can be handled without touching the surface.

▲ For fine lines and better definition, use any steel implement with a suitable point to remove the varnish. The area free of varnish will be etched by the acid.

Mordants

The most commonly used acids are hydrochloric acid (HCl), nitric acid (HNO₃), and sulfuric acid (H₂SO₄). Their primary advantage is that they all mix with water.

Use these proportions when preparing acid etching baths:

Metal	Nitric Acid	Hydrochloric Acid	Distilled Water
Gold	1 part	3 parts	40 parts
Silver	1 part		3–4 parts
Copper	1 part		1–2 parts

The solution of one part nitric acid to three parts hydrochloric acid is called *aqua regia*. Acid should always be added to the water, rather than adding water to acid, to avoid a violent reaction.

Acid is heavier than water; shake the mixture gently so that the etching will act evenly over the entire piece.

The Etching Process

The concentration of acid, time, and temperature are all factors that influence the final result of the etched piece.

Always use good quality acids free of impurities. A high concentration of acid reduces the amount of time the metal needs to stay in the acid. It is harder to control the result when the acid concentration is high, but the effects can be very interesting. Pay close attention when using high concentrations because they can cause the varnish to lift off. A more diluted solution produces well-defined lines.

An important factor is temperature. The amount of time needed for an etching is influenced by the temperature of the solution; higher temperatures require less time. Time, too, is another basic factor. The more time the metal is in contact with the mordant, the deeper the etching.

How to Etch

Always use a heat-resistant, glass container for etching with acid, primarily because the mixture of acid and water produces heat, but it also allows the option of heating the container itself, in order to accelerate the etching process.

➤ This silver piece by Carles Codina was etched with a very strong acid. The result is a less defined design, but one that is in keeping with the overall intended effect.

Use plastic or wooden tongs when putting a piece in the acid bath. Remove it more easily from the bottom of the bath by crossing two cotton strings underneath the piece and hanging the ends over the sides of the container. Monitor the depth of the etching by putting a test piece of metal next to the working piece. After etching, remove the varnish with a brush and solvent.

▲ This piece by Sabine Meinke exhibits the results of slow etching in a weaker acid solution.

▲ Controlling the three factors of acid strength, temperature, and time, ensures a well-crafted etching. It is possible to compensate for a weak acid solution by increasing either the time or the temperature.

▼ Here is the result of two different effects from the same acid bath. The metal piece with the more deeply etched design was in the bath longer than the one with the less defined written script.

▲ Use etching to create textures on volumetric pieces. Here the piece was heated slightly and red flake shellac sprinkled on through a sieve so that the shellac fused to the metal. The piece was then etched in acid.

➤ The shellac acted as a resist to the acid, creating this interesting texture.

Safety Measures

Etching acids are dangerous. They damage nasal membranes when inhaled and cause serious burns when they come into contact with the skin; always work with them using special gloves, a respirator, and protective goggles. The work place should be well-ventilated and the acids kept in a safe place.

Combining Metals

Precious metals can be joined with solder, but it is also possible to fuse metals together without solder by submitting them to high temperatures, a reduction atmosphere, and pressure. The following section presents two techniques for combining metals; the methods are distinctly different. First we will look at the technique of *mokume gane*, which is a fusion technique, and then we will examine a simple twisted union using solder.

Mokume Gane

This technique was used 300 years ago for making sword furniture. In Japanese, mokume means "wood grain" and gane means "metal." The name probably was coined because the finished product looks similar to laminated wood. Mokume gane consists of metal sheets made into a laminated block. A block can be made with solder or with diffusion welding. Fusion is a more complicated technique, but the results are far superior. Furthermore, since there is no solder to eliminate afterwards, working the block is much easier.

Preparing the Billet

The first step is to make a solid block or *billet* of metal by submitting the sheets to intense heat in a reduction atmosphere under pressure so that the metals join together without the use of solder. For this we prepare special alloyed sheets of different precious metals, the key to which is their copper content. The amount of copper added to the metals changes the fusing points so that they are all very close to one another no matter what precious metal they contain. Their hardness is then also similar, and once the sheets fuse they are compatible when forged and rolled.

Table A lists the different alloys used in mokume gane.

▼ Table A: Alloys

	Fine gold	Silver	Copper
Shakudo	4.8%	-	95.2%
	2.5%	-	97.5%
Shibuichi	-	40%	60%
	-	30%	70%
Shiro-shibuichi	-	60%	40%

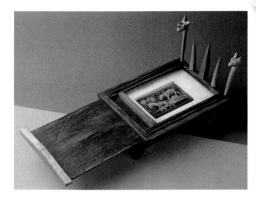

▲ For *Dark Dead Grass Steps for Tomorrow*, artist Judith McCaig etched and chased the metal, then combined different sheets of gold on silver.

Combine these alloys with each other in different proportions. For example, combining *shakudo* and *shibuichi* in the proportions indicated in Table B, makes an alloy called *kuro-shibuichi*.

▼ Table B: How to obtain the alloy kuro-shibuichi

Shakudo + Shibuichi
83.3% + 16.7%
71.4% + 28.6%
58.8% + 41.2%

Alternate the alloyed sheets to achieve contrasts in tone, remembering that the alloys with the highest copper content will change color over time.

In this example, we have placed a sheet of pure gold on top and a thicker copper sheet on the bottom.

➤ 4. Next, arrange the clamp plates as shown in the photo and tie securely with thick binding wire. These plates ensure uniform pressure on the entire surface.

➤ 5. Either a coal forge or an oven of charcoal bricks may be used to create the heat reduction atmosphere. When the box turns red orange, apply pressure to the unit with an old hammer and melting tongs. Sweating or shimmering at the edges of the metal sheets indicates that the billet has fused.

▲ 1. Make sure that the sheets are perfectly flat and well sanded so that there are no surface irregularities. Once this is done, clean them first with water and baking soda, and then with alcohol, taking care not to touch the sheets with the fingers.

▲ 2. Even though scale will form on the clamp plates, it is important to paint both sides of the plates that will come into contact with the sheets, using a solder inhibitor.

▲ 3. Place six sheets of metal within the clamp plates and cover with a very diluted borax/water solution.

Rolling

After making the billet, forge it on an anvil with a steel hammer in order to compact the metal before rolling it.

▼ 1. Once the billet is pickled and cleaned, it should look like the example shown here. The different layers of metal are visible; note the absence of solder. This billet is now like one solid piece of metal.

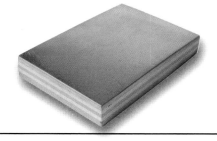

▲ 2. Forge the billet and then roll it until it has been reduced to half its original thickness.

▲ 3. Cut the sheet in half, sand and clean the surfaces of the two halves as before; then put them back in the box of clamp plates and fuse them again.

➤ 4. Now the billet contains 12 layers. This process of rolling and fusing can be repeated as often as desired.

Working the Billet

Try different ways of working the fused billet, such as drilling holes with different sized drill bits before or after rolling. In the following example, we filed wide crosswise grooves.

▲ 1. If the billet is thick enough, varying the width and depth of the grooves will produce different effects in the rolling stage.

▲ 2. Once filed, the grooves produce surprising effects when forged and rolled. After the thickness of the billet is reduced, the same grooves can be filed again for more depth.

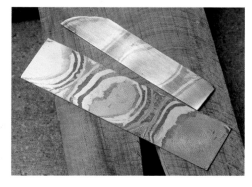

▲ 3. Roll the billet until it becomes a thin sheet. The grooves appear as a gradation of stripes across the sheet.

▼ Even without cuts or penetrations in the billet, the sheet can be worked in many different ways.

▼ Instead of grooves cut only in one direction, try cutting in both directions to make a square pattern.

▼ Cutting and drilling the billet yields various effects.

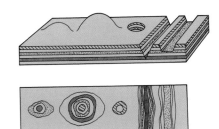

Twisting

Metal bars and rolled sheets are made by twisting together gold and silver wires, or any combination of the alloys used in mokume gane. There is no limit to the variety of creative possibilities inherent in this technique.

▲ Brooch and earrings by Francesco Pavan

Making a Metal Sheet

Twist and roll wires of different types of metal together to create unique metal sheets of varying chromatic ranges.

➤ 2. Here a variety of gold and silver wires were annealed and pickled. Any of the alloys mentioned in the section on mokume gane can be used, as well as different combinations of colored gold.

◄ 1. Using a hand drill, twist together one wire of gold with one of silver. Solder them together at one end and insert them into the drill chuck, holding them together at the other end with a pair of pliers, while turning the drill handle until the wires are firmly twisted.

▲ 3. Here is one option for combining the twisted wires using five twists of two wires each with a solder wire in the center. Tie the group of wires together with binding wire and apply flux before heating.

◄ 4. Another method is to tie smooth wire of different metals with binding wire and solder in the same way as above. It's important that the wires are bound tightly so as to minimize the amount of solder that gets between them. Too much solder creates undesirable yellow areas in the rolled sheet.

▲ 5. Rings can be made by twisting wires together and then drawing them with a wire drawbench, to give them a round or square shape suitable for a ring. In this photo we are soldering rolled rectangular wires together to make a sheet.

▼ 6. Remove excess solder from the surface by filing the rolled sheet on both sides with a coarse file.

▼ Bracelet by Stefano Marchetti

➤ 7. Continue rolling the sheet to a thickness of .6 mm. To obtain a higher contrast, oxidize it with a silver oxidizer. Remember to use hard solder at this stage if more solder will be needed later to finish the piece.

Simple Ring

Using three wires and only one solder joint, this ring is easy to make.

➤ 1. Put the ends of two or three wires together in a vice and twist the other end to form a wire like the one shown.

◄ 2. Shape the ring with a mandrel and solder the ends. A bath of silver oxidizer darkens only the silver; it has no effect on gold.

Chain with Forged Links

We demonstrated how to make this chain in the section on jump rings.

The only difference here is that the links are made of two different metals—gold and silver.

▲ 1. Make two rectangular wires and solder them with hard solder. Roll and draw them in a rectangular wire drawplate.

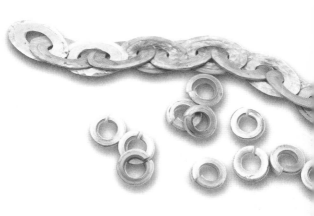

◄ 3. Oxidize the bracelet to augment the contrast between the silver and the gold.

▲ 2. Once annealed, make jump rings as previously shown. After soldering, roll and forge them with a hammer, then join them together.

Gold and Silver Ring without Solder

Make this ring using only the properties inherent in the metals to bond them, without using solder.

➤ 1. Roll and polish a metal sheet of silver. On the surface, place various pieces of fine gold dipped in flux.

▲ 2. Heat the metal evenly with a torch, turning it periodically until the gold fuses to the silver.

▲ 3. Roll the metal to a thickness of .8 mm and polish.

▲ 4. Use a mandrel to shape the ring, then solder the ends.

➤ 5. The ring is shown here after oxidizing the silver.

Granulation

Granulation is fusing very small balls of gold or silver, either to themselves or to a metal surface, without using solder. In fact, it is possible to make balls so small that they resemble grains of sand. Etruscan works of the 6th and 5th centuries B.C. are good examples of this technique.

Metal Granules

A granule is the basic element of this technique. Eighteen-karat gold or sterling silver can be granulated, but granules of pure gold and silver work better because their fusing temperature is higher and the process can be controlled more easily. Once the granulation process is finished, the surface will appear lighter, and it will be difficult to see the points of contact. Working with unalloyed metals requires the application of copper in a chemical or solid form.

When a metal melts, it naturally draws up into the most efficient of forms, that of a sphere. These metal spheres can be made using pieces of wire, jump rings, or paillons. In order to achieve the best granulated effect, the granules must be completely round. The first step consists of preparing the metal so that it will produce a round shape. Two ways of doing this are demonstrated here.

▲ This ring by Harold O'Connor uses granulation to create a new look in jewelry.

Preparing the Metal

Method 1:

Cut small paillons of metal and place them on a block of charcoal for heating. A small number of granules can be made quickly using this procedure. There are better methods for greater quantities.

Method 2:

To make balls of equal weight and size, make wire jump rings on a mandrel

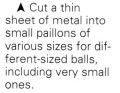

▲ Cut a thin sheet of metal into small paillons of various sizes for different-sized balls, including very small ones.

◄ Granulated rings by Carles Codina

as previously explained. Jump rings cut from the same coil will produce balls of exactly the same size. Then make small concave holes in a charcoal block using a round bur. Place jump rings in each hole so that when they melt and form into balls, they will hold their spherical shape and not roll around.

Making the Granules

For both methods described above, once the balls form, let them cool; then pickle, and then let them dry. If spheres are made using a hard soldering block, the shape will not be perfectly round, especially on the side that was in contact with the block. It is important to use a charcoal block because it maintains a more uniform and longer lasting heat than other types of blocks.

To make a larger quantity of granules at one time, use a lost wax casting mold. First, put a layer of coarsely ground charcoal inside the mold, then spread a layer of very finely ground charcoal atop that. Place the pieces of metal or jump rings on top of the fine charcoal so that they are not

▼ Here jump rings of very fine silver wire are each placed in holes in the block. The great advantage of using jump rings is that each one weighs exactly the same and will form balls of identical size.

touching each other. The purpose of the bed of fine charcoal is to prevent the pieces from shifting and fusing together. Fill the mold with as many pieces of metal as will fit, so long as they do not touch.

Seal the mold with a refractory clay and place it in an oven at a temperature higher than the melting point of the metal. The amount of oven time required depends on the type of metal and the size of the mold.

Granulating Solutions

In the process of granulation a minimal join takes place, enabling the ball to join to another metal surface. For this to happen, the point of contact between the metal elements must be heated; this thermal reaction breaks down the crystalline structures of the metals. It is at this point that the presence of copper in the granulating solution becomes vital: the copper penetrates both metals so that their melting point at the point of contact on the exterior is lower than their interior melting point. The ball can then join with another metal element without melting entirely.

There are many different kinds of granulating solutions, but they all contain two indispensable elements: copper and carbon. For copper, use solid copper or any of the following copper salts: copper hydroxide, copper chloride, copper acetate, black copper oxide, or red copper oxide.

To make red copper, submerge the granules in old acid, together with steel wire, until the balls turn light red. An alternative method involves placing the balls in an 460°C oven so that they oxidize when removed.

For the carbon, use any colloidal organic binder which emits carbon when burned, such as fish glue, gum tragacanth, gum arabic, or any white glue used for handicrafts, as long as it contains only organic substances.

▲ Grind the charcoal using a mortar and pestle and then sift to separate the fine from the coarse.

▼ Use a charcoal block without holes to melt very small pieces of metal. After heat is applied directly with a soldering torch, the metal will form itself into balls and roll off the block into the container of water. To avoid thermal shock, which will cause them to deform, let them cool slightly first.

▲ Make granules by cutting small pieces of fine metal and putting them in separate holes in a charcoal block. Then, using a soldering torch, apply heat until they melt. Once they take on the shape of balls, let them cool, then pickle in acid.

▼ Some of the granulating solutions are complex and laborious to prepare but give excellent results. The green solution shown below, called cupric oxide, is commonly used.

Granulation on a Flat Ring

Sort the granules according to size. Although balls of different sizes may be joined, the best results come from balls that are well-rounded and similar in size.

Either put the solution on both the ball and the surface to be granulated, or only on the ball, bearing in mind that an excess of solution, just as an excess of copper, can negatively affect the fusion process.

To place the granules, use tweezers, wooden spatulas or, as shown here, a paintbrush.

Apply a reducing flame and work as quickly as possible, without removing the flame from the piece for even a moment. Use a charcoal block, because an even distribution of heat is essential in this process.

➤ 3. Place a small amount of solution in another container and submerge the granules in it just before placing them on the ring.

▼ 5. Heat can be applied with an oven or a torch. The heat forms the weld rapidly, so pay close attention that the piece does not melt.

Once the granules have bonded, pickle in acid to eliminate oxidation.

▲ 1. Use strainers of different sizes to sort the balls. Here, various sizes of coffee (percolator) filters are an economical alternative.

▲ 2. This is a solution of black copper oxide and gum arabic, with a bit of boric salt added for the proper consistency.

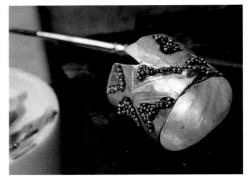

▲ 4. Drying is one of the most important stages in the process. Let one side dry before attempting to place more balls on other sides, or the heat from the torch may displace the granules.

▼ Granulation on a ring by Carles Codina

▲ After granulation has been applied, additional techniques may be used. Granulated rings by Carles Codina

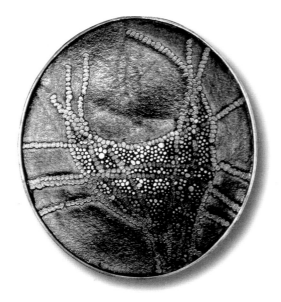

▲ The granules may be flattened with a hammer, or filed down for further effects. Granulated brooch by Harold O'Connor

Granulation without a Base

It is possible to join the granules to one another without an underlying support surface. To make the ring shown here, Verónica Andrade used large granules of pure silver. She used the same solution described earlier, but the larger balls required one of thicker consistency.

◄ Granulated silver bowl by David Huycke

▲ 2. When the lateral units are finished, solder them together in an open square formation.

◄ 1. Make 1.5mm granules and cover them in granulating solution as described earlier. Construct the four lateral units and lay them on a piece of mica to keep them from adhering to the base. When they are dry, apply heat to fuse the balls, being careful not to move them out of place.

◄ 3. Make a gold ring to solder into the inside of the square. They should fit perfectly, one inside the other.

➤ 4. Once the two elements are joined, use silver oxidizer to darken the granulated silver, as in this granulated ring of gold and silver by Verónica Andrade.

Creating Textures

The flat surfaces of milled sheets are well-suited for the creation of reliefs and textures using *chisels*, *burins*, etching acids—such a variety of tools and materials are available that the range of possibilities is infinite. This section discusses various ways of creating texture mechanically, using the impact of a hammer and the pressure of a rolling mill.

◀ Textured ring by Silke Knetsch

▲ Some methods of adding texture to metal involve wax and other materials that melt. A wax impression created this texture on a brooch by Carles Codina.

Hammered Texture

One of the tools that offers the most possibilities for creating texture is the hammer. Not only does the type and shape of the hammer make a difference, but so does the working surface under the piece. The

▼ Hammering works best on annealed metal.

look of hammering can be distinctively different, depending upon whether the metal is hammered on top of a steel base, a lead base, or a sandbag. As is true with forging, if a sheet of metal is hit on steel, the sheet expands outward. If it is hit on a soft surface, however, it will change into another shape entirely.

Use new hammers or modify old hammers by notching the surfaces so that the impression of the notch is left on the metal. Changes in cadence, rhythm, and

orientation while hammering will also create very different results, even when using the same hammer.

You can also make different punches using steel rods, old file handles, and the like. In the section on chasing, we will describe how to make a punch, although to create different textures it is not necessary they all be of the same temper.

▼ The narrow end of a hammer is used on silver disks. Earrings by Beatriz Würsch

Embossing with a Rolling Mill

Embossing patterns and designs onto metal is simple when using the extreme pressure of a rolling mill, which can imprint many kinds of textures onto sheet metal.

To imprint a design from a very hard sheet of metal (such as nickel silver or a thin sheet of stainless steel), put the sheet of silver or gold on top and a brass sheet underneath to keep the harder object from coming into contact with the rollers. Use this method to imprint textures from materials as diverse as paper, cardboard, or plastic.

➤ The textured material should pass between two sheets of brass, especially if using steel or any material that could damage the rollers.

▲ In this example, pieces of saw blade were rolled between two sheets of silver. The interior of one set of impressions was oxidized. The steel penetrated deeply into the thick sheet of annealed silver.

◀ Abrasive papers can create many textures on metal.

➤ Stiff paper such as cardboard leaves a pleasing impression on a sheet of annealed silver.

▲ This texture is the result of rolling the metal with a crumpled sheet of paper.

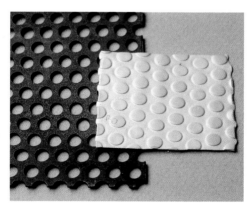

▲ A piece of perforated steel screen leaves a precise impression on the silver sheet. The circles are slightly oval—a deformity due to the stretching caused by the roller. The embossing is never exactly the same as the original.

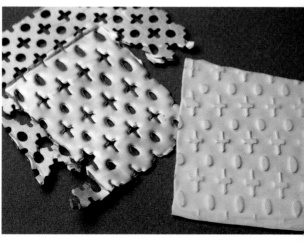

▲ Patterned aluminum also leaves an impression, but the imprint is greatly deformed in comparison to the original, because of aluminum's softness.

Reticulation

Reticulation dates back to the Victorian period in Czarist Russia and Scandinavia. Fabergé was one of the most renowned artists to work with this technique, creating a multitude of objects such as card cases, spectacle cases, and liquor flasks.

This process creates a surface texture of crests and valleys through its distinctive method of heating and cooling the metal. The procedure leaves the top surface of a sheet of silver-copper alloy richer in silver than the interior layer, so that the interior layer, containing more copper, has a lower melting point than the surface. This difference in melting points makes the sheet deform when heat is applied, somewhat like a bag of water, because only the inner layer melts. As this happens, a solid layer of copper oxide forms between the layers. When the interior cools, the melted metal contracts and pushes against the layer of copper oxide, forming crests on the surface which create an effect that resembles very aged skin.

▲ A reticulated sheet, after darkening the deep creases with a silver oxidizing agent

Preparing the Sheet

To create a silver-rich exterior surface, heat the sheet and then eliminate the copper generated on the surface with up to a 33% sulfuric acid solution. The elimination of surface copper creates an exterior surface that is practically pure silver—nearly 1,000 fine—and therefore having a higher melting point.

Heat the silver by placing the sheet in a 650°C oven or kiln for 10 minutes. Pickle the sheet in a sulfuric acid/water solution and scratch brush the surface. Repeat this process at least four times, after which the sheet will be a dead white as a result of having almost all the copper eliminated from the surface. When using a blowpipe torch, heat the sheet until the oxidation appears, and follow that by pickling it in new acid, repeating this process at least five times. Fine silver can be reticulated, but it is best to use silver with a high copper content, such as 800–820 parts per thousand.

Applying Heat

Reticulation is a process that requires practice, and the results are somewhat unpredictable; therefore, start with a sheet that is larger than the size actually needed, so that a selection can be made from the area with the most interesting texture.

◄ 1. Begin with a smooth sheet of silver 820 fine, no less than .5 mm thick. The surface should be clean and free of scratches.

▼ 2. To eliminate the surface oxide, prepare a new solution of pickling acid that is stronger than usual.

▼ 3. To make the reticulation even more pronounced, put steel nails and thumbtacks between the metal and the charcoal block. These will act as heat sinks, absorbing more heat than the block and aiding the reticulation process.

▲ 1. As the sheet heats up, the interior melts because the melting point is lower in the center than on the surface. The exterior surface, which is rich in silver, remains solid.

▲ 2. It is best to start the process with a medium flame, and increase the size of the flame as the metal begins to collapse. After this happens, pass the flame along the entire surface of the sheet. Varying flame temperature has different effects on the metal.

▲ 3. During the application of heat, tensions are released in the metal for various reasons, the most important of which is temperature; this melts the interior and makes the metal expand. When the metal cools and contracts, the exterior surface conforms to the contracted inner structure, making the surface rough. Reticulated metal is porous and difficult to solder, so it is best to use cold-joining techniques, such as rivets or screws.

After the piece is completely sanded, choose the final finish. Although there are many to choose from, one of the most common is a *mirror finish*.

A mirror finish, like any other good finish, requires that the surface be perfect. It must have been properly fabricated, then correctly sanded so that all scratches have been eliminated. If the surface is not in optimum condition, the desired result will be difficult to attain.

While there are several different techniques for giving metal a mirror finish, this section concentrates on manual polishing, done with a *buffing motor*, because it gives the best results.

▼Though they are not polished to a mirror finish, the finish on these gold earrings with aquamarine by Sandel Kerpen is nonetheless exquisite.

Polishing and Buffing Tools

A buffing motor is essential for a mirror finish. Its attachments—polishing wheels of different shapes, various widths of brushes, *muslin wheels*, and an assortment of *buffs*—fit onto the chucks of the motor. As a general rule, use two sets for each of the two stages: polishing and buffing.

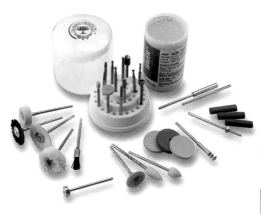

▲ Use the buffing motor at 2,800–3,000 rpm for the best results. There are many attachments available that fit on the two chucks.

◀Flexible shaft motors and micro motors also have an extensive range of polishing and buffing attachments especially designed for accessing corners, interiors, and stone settings, or for working with delicate pieces.

➤ Certain types of disks do not require polishing or buffing compounds, and permit fine precision polishing. These disks are used for small, tight, hard-to-reach places inaccessible to the buffing motor.

➤ To polish rings, stone settings, corners, and other hard-to-reach places, use thrumming threads impregnated with a polishing or buffing compound.

A Mirror Shine

There are two essential steps in the process of achieving a mirror shine: *polishing* and *buffing*. Polishing consists of eliminating all marks left by sanding, using a rougher, more abrasive polishing compound; buffing achieves the definitive brilliance using softer, gentler buffing compounds.

The Process

Normally, polishing is done with *compounds* made of either *tripoli* or pumice powder and wax, which acts as a binder. These compounds take off some of the metal and give a slight shine to the piece.

Study the piece carefully before beginning to polish, and choose the appropriate tools. In order not to round off edges, use hard wheels for flat shapes and natural bristle brushes for rounded shapes. After completing the polishing, clean the piece thoroughly before buffing.

Buffing essentially repeats the same process done in polishing, but uses softer buffing compounds, such as green or red rouge, which do not remove metal. Finally, polish the piece with a muslin buffing wheel, wash it, then put it in clean sawdust to dry. The sawdust will eliminate every trace of humidity.

▼ Before polishing, make sure there are no scratches on the piece from prior sanding. Use emery paper to remove them before using the buffing motor. Execute each step thoroughly before moving on to the next.

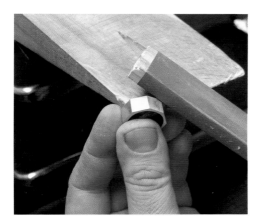

Polishing Flat Surfaces

In order to polish flat surfaces without rounding off the edges, sand each plane carefully before polishing and use a flat, felt polishing wheel. Brush disks and other attachments damage the edges, so avoid using them.

➤ 1. Apply a polishing compound to the felt wheel. This is the first of several compounds needed.

▲ 2. To polish this octagonal ring, use a flat wheel to avoid rounding off the edges. Always use the inner portion of the wheel, moving the piece slightly to change the direction of surface contact with the wheel.

▲ 3. To polish the interior of a ring, use a felt inside-ring buff. As the buff turns, rotate the ring in all directions.

▲ 4. Next, polish the sides in the same way. Clean the piece with hot water and soap, or in an ultrasonic cleaner before changing to a buffing compound.

➤ 5. To buff, repeat steps 1–4 using a separate set of buffing wheels and compounds, such as red rouge. Buffing will give the piece its definitive mirror finish.

◀ 6. Create the final shine using a muslin buffing wheel and some red rouge.

➤ 7. Even though the shine can be refined still further with different attachments and specific products, avoid using too much compound.

Polishing Curved Forms

These kinds of shapes require special brushes because hard wheels leave small planed areas that are difficult to remove in the final finish.

➤ 1. Sometimes flap wheel brushes made with strips of synthetic household scouring pads can leave a very nice polished surface.

➤ 3. Next, after cleaning, buff it with a muslin wheel and red rouge, using only the minimum necessary. Constantly turn the piece in all directions during buffing.

➤➤ 4. It can be dangerous to polish chains with a buffing motor. Always extend a chain over a block of wood as a safety precaution.

➤ 2. To polish a curved form like the one shown here, a narrow black brush is ideal for polishing hard-to-reach places. Be sure to move the piece in all directions so that the brush will not leave marks.

Cleaning

Polishing requires working with care; always keep the polishing and buffing attachments clean. Keep them separated according to their function, and never mix compounds. Take special care with buffing equipment, because a dirty or worn buffing wheel can defeat the purpose.

Before moving on from polishing to buffing, completely remove all traces of polishing compound from the piece. Do this by using hot water and some degreasing liquid detergent. Rub the piece with a soft brush until it is clean.

Other Finishing Methods

Matte and satin finishes are most commonly oxidized with heat, and then pickled with acid. Another possibility is sandblasting, which is often used for satin finishes. A *sandblaster* is a small machine that uses air pressure to expel very fine grains of sand or glass beads for a finely textured matte surface.

▲ One easy way to create a satin finish is to rub the surface with a household scouring pad. Either rub the surface while it is dry or use water and baking soda to produce more of a shine.

◄ The steel wires of this buffing motor attachment strike the surface of the piece, giving it a matte finish similar to sandblasting.

➤ An ultrasonic cleaner is a very practical machine used not only to eliminate polishing compounds, but also to clean gems and other materials.

▼ Acids can also add shine to the final finish, augmenting the effect and color of gold, as seen in this bracelet by Carles Codina.

Patination

When metal is exposed to air and humidity, a natural process of oxidation occurs. In the case of bronze sculptures that have been exposed to the elements, this effect turns the metal to a greenish *patina* over time. Oxidation is very attractive in jewelry and sculpture simply as an overall patina or to highlight depth in a piece. Oxidation is a natural reaction, and this section shows how to accelerate and modify this reaction to obtain different patinas. It can also give new work the look of antiquity in a short span of time.

The strongest and most varied patinas are best achieved with metals having a high copper content in the alloy. For this reason, gold is difficult to oxidize but silver oxidizes easily, although only in tones of gray and black. The greatest range of patinas is possible using metals, such as copper, bronze, and brass.

➤ There are various factors that influence the oxidation process. Heating and cooling accelerate it, but the patina itself is determined by the proportion of diverse chemical products, and the way in which they are applied to the metal.

◄ Oxidation is a natural phenomena. Most bronze objects naturally acquire interesting patinas as they are exposed to the elements over time. This often occurs in ethnic jewelry, such as this bronze choker from Zaire.

▼ This bronze piece, by Francesc Guitart, was colored by successive applications and heat sets of potassium sulfide, iron nitrate, and titanium dioxide.

that it produces oxides when it dries. Alternate spraying patina formulas with spraying distilled water, for maximum control of the patina.

Immersion

Suspend the piece in a glass container or heat-resistant vessel or pot, and heat according to the patina formula directions. The boiling and immersion times are very important to obtain a good patina.

Fuming

Suspend the piece, together with a piece of cotton soaked in the patina formula, inside a glass container that can be hermetically sealed. This creates an atmosphere that produces an even, overall coloring with no spotting, especially in small pieces that contain a combination of copper or bronze with metals such as silver and gold. Tightly seal the container, making sure the cotton does not come in contact with the piece; there should be no direct contact between the chemical and the metal. Catch the edge of the cotton with the lid of the container, or make an interior support for it.

Ways to Apply Patinas

In this section we will explain five of the most useful and interesting ways to apply chemical coloring products: spraying, immersion, *fuming*, contact patination, and heat application.

Spraying

Spraying is a practical and easy application method for large pieces. Use different spray bottles for each patina to be used, and another one for distilled water. Spray a fine film of the patina formula, so

Patina-Soaked Sawdust

Surround the piece with sawdust saturated in the patina, so that it oxidizes on contact with the sawdust. This method produces a characteristic spotting. Changing the size and type of sawdust will vary the effects.

Heat

Submerge the piece in a patina, apply it with a brush or a folded cotton cloth, or rub it gently on the surface. Then heat the piece with a soldering torch, or place it in an oven.

Patinas

A multitude of patinas may be created on copper and bronze because there are so many chemicals available and so many metal alloys possible—these all influence the final result. The patinas that follow have simple formulas and easy-to-find ingredients, are simple to make, and are not especially hazardous. All of these patinas can be applied using the methods just described.

Blue Green

This is the most frequently used patina and there are several ways to obtain it. Ammonia salts (which can be found in most pharmacies) are particularly useful for larger pieces. Dissolve the salts in distilled water and apply a fine layer of spray

▼ Brooch with several different patinas by Carles Codina

◄ According to the size and composition of the sawdust, the effect on the surface can vary considerably.

▲Note how contact with pieces of the sawdust dotted the surface of this piece with color.

on the surface of the piece. Once it has dried in the sun, apply another layer, but this time use only distilled water. Alternate the ammonia salt solution with the distilled water, repeating as often as necessary to achieve the desired tone. The process can be sped up by heating the piece, but the tones are of better quality when it is left to dry in the sun, and the ammonia salts are applied in several light layers. Too high a concentration of ammonia salts can cause the patina to come off.

The results are greatly improved when a somewhat roughly textured surface is used, whether obtained by some mechanical method or by using acid.

Yellowish accents on green patina, or an overall yellow, comes from using a high concentration of iron sulfate in water, either by immersion or spraying. The variation of tone depends on how much iron sulfate is in the solution.

A similar effect is possible by mixing 100 g of copper nitrate and 40 cc of a 70% nitric acid solution into 1 liter of water. It is best to heat this application with a soldering torch.

▲ Green tones

▼ This bronze piece, by Francesc Guitart, has been colored using potassium sulfate, copper nitrate, and iron nitrate. They were applied in that order, and heated with a blowpipe torch after each application.

Violet

A violet tone can be made from a solution of 200 g of copper nitrate in 1 liter of water. Bring the solution to a boil, then put the piece in it for 20 minutes. Finally, wash and dry the piece.

Like many others, this patina can be applied with a spray bottle; you can also use the sawdust method, and set it with a soldering torch. The effect will be quite different and the tone much greener.

▼ Violet patina from copper nitrate

Dark Orange

To make dark orange tones use a dilution of 120 g of copper sulfate in 1 liter of water to which is added 30 cc of ammonia. Use this solution the same day as it is prepared, because ammonia is unstable and will lose its potency. Apply this solution as a hot immersion bath. Let the solution come to a boil before immersing the piece for 20 minutes. Then wash the piece with plenty of water and let it dry in the sun. Do not handle it until it is completely dry.

Red Orange

For yellower tones of orange mix a solution of 50 g of copper sulfate, 5 g of iron sulfate, 5 g of zinc sulfate, and 25 g of potassium permanganate in 1 liter of water.

Make sure each chemical is completely diluted before adding the next, and apply it as a hot immersion bath. Submerge the piece in the boiling solution for two minutes, then take it out and clean the black layer that has formed. Repeat this operation if the black layer forms again, keeping the piece in the boiling solution for 20 minutes. This patina varies according to the composition of the bronze used.

◄ Note how the previous acid etching work enhances these maroon–orange tones.

Matte Black

Dilute 5 g of potassium permanganate, 50 g of copper sulfate, and 5 g of iron sulfate in 1 liter of water. When the solution is boiling, submerge the piece for 20 minutes, then wash it with water and let it dry without handling it.

Dark Red

For a dark red tone, use a solution of 10 g of iron nitrate in 1 liter of water, and apply with a paintbrush. After setting the patina with a soldering torch, apply another layer so that it will be even. Finally, seal the patina with a layer of wax.

For a more orange-maroon tone, use a solution made with 25 g of copper sulfate, between 3–5 cc of ammonia, and 1 liter of water. Use as a boiling immersion bath.

◄ This black patina changed from matte to an intense shine when wax was applied as a final finish.

▼ Orange tones can be made in more than one way.

Aging Effects on Metal

This process gives an aged appearance to a new piece of bronze or other metal with a high copper content.

Begin with a brief pickling in nitric acid and water and brush it vigorously to eliminate surface oxidation. Soak sawdust in a solution of nitric acid and water. Put the bronze in a large glass or wooden container, and cover it with the sawdust. The outcome will depend a lot upon the concentration of acid—the more acid in the solution, the greater the effect. Following this, put the piece in a patina-soaked sawdust.

A variation of this method is to saturate the nitric acid with copper by placing a piece of copper in the acid. Take the copper out when it exhibits a bluish-green tinge, indicating the acid is completely saturated but still active. Soak sawdust in this acid, which is now copper nitrate. Since the acid is still active, the sawdust will give the piece an antique finish.

Experience is the key to obtaining good patina finishes. The fineness of the sawdust and the active concentration of the acid are factors than can affect the outcome. Better results are achieved when the sawdust and the acid are not uniformly mixed, so that the effect is random. If some areas of the piece come in contact with the acid more than others, the aging effect looks more realistic.

To vary the look even more, use an unevenly saturated fine sawdust and shake the container or move the piece slightly after several hours, so that the acid works on the metal differently in different places. The green tone that results will intensify when dried in the sun and sealed in wax.

➤ After being heat-dried, protect the oxide with a special metal lacquer, as seen here on *Endangered Species No. 2* by Carles Codina.

◄ Repeated oxidation of the foreground and background created this effect on Judith McCaig's *Dream Whalers*.

Oxidizing Silver

Silver oxidizes naturally to a grayish black tone by contact with air and humidity. It also blackens from surface oxidization when heated and then cooled.

Silver may be oxidized with commercial products, but it is a simple matter—and more economical—to make the oxide. Potassium sulfate is the most common, made by dissolving 30 g of sulfate in 1 liter of hot water and then adding 8 g of ammonia, which turns the solution a deeper black. Sulfate loses its potency easily, so store it in an airtight, light-proof container.

Before using the oxidizer, make sure the surface of the silver is completely clean and pickled. Homemade oxidizers must be warmed to obtain the best quality and set of the patina. When using a brush, use one made of synthetic bristles, because the solution will destroy natural fibers. The results are best on annealed silver.

▼ The best way to apply an oxidizing agent is to submerge the piece with a copper or silver wire.

Maintain the sulfate solution in a hot bath. First heat the piece by submerging it in boiling water, then put it in the sulfate, and then back in the water again. Take out the piece immediately and hold it in the vapor of the boiling water to set the patina. Once oxidized, rinse and dry the piece, then apply a metal lacquer.

To patina only the background of a piece, first oxidize it overall and, once fixed, polish or rub the relief surface until the silver shows through again.

Green Patinated Brooch

This easy technique makes interesting objects. Wax, discussed later in the section on lost wax casting (page 116), aids in making an impression of textures, such as those shown here.

This brooch was made by taking impressions in clay of an assortment of materials using varying degrees of pressure. The design was then translated into bronze using a technique that is as ancient as the art of jewelry making itself—lost wax casting.

➤ Carefully select the materials for the textured impressions. They should be durable, with well-defined texture, so that the marks left in the clay will be clear and precise. Some of these are found objects and some have been specially made out of wood.

◄ To make the wax mold, use a small piece of clay and pink dental wax.

◄ 2. To make a mold that will hold the wax when it is poured over the design, add a lip of clay around the edge.

▲ 1. Make a flat slab of clay by hand or with the help of a rolling pin. Make impressions on the surface, using a variety of objects and materials.

➤ 3. Melt the wax slowly without boiling it and then pour it into the clay mold, making sure it flows evenly into all the nooks and crannies of the design. Let it cool for a few minutes. The wax in direct contact with the clay will cool the fastest. After taking the wax out of the mold, trim off the excess wax that is still hot.

◄ 5. Completely clean the wax piece, then follow the instructions in the section on lost wax casting (page 116) to create the piece in bronze. If the proper equipment for the procedure is not available, send it to a casting specialist.

➤ 6. Pickle the bronze piece in an equal solution of nitric acid and water to eliminate oxidation. Submerge the piece in the solution for just a few moments.

▲ 4. Very carefully lift out the wax and trim the excess with a scalpel. Use a soft brush to clean off any clay particles that may be stuck to the wax.

▲ 7. Here the piece has been pickled, cleaned, and dried. Avoid all contact with impurities, especially oils from the hands.

◄ 8. Apply the first layer of ammonia salts with a spray bottle, so that the surface is thoroughly wet. Put it in the sun to dry.

➤ 9. After the first application, continue the process, alternating the application of ammonia salts with one of distilled water, and letting it dry thoroughly between each application.

◄ 10. Each layer will create a more intense shade of green, but too much solution can cause the patina to flake off.

▲ 11. For a yellower tone, prepare a clear solution of iron sulfate and water, and submerge the piece for a moment, then let it dry.

▲12. The piece cannot be soldered, because excess heat will destroy the patina, so the piece will be screw mounted on this backing.

▲ 13. The pin is made with a steel wire, using pliers to bend it double. This kind of closure is appropriate for a large brooch because it fastens securely to the clothing, preventing it from hanging forward.

▲14. Use a stiff brush to remove the patina from the relief surface, for a more realistic look. Apply wax with a folded cloth and let the piece dry.

➤ Brooch by Ramón Puíg Cuyàs

In this chapter are demonstrated some crafts that exist independently of jewelry making but have been used by jewelers for centuries and now are considered part of a jeweler's repertoire.

Chasing and repoussé make it possible to give a flat sheet of metal both volume and decorative interest. Enameling and Japanese lacquer amplify the chromatic range available in jewelry. The particularly specialized techniques of gem setting and lost wax casting are also included here.

Today, jewelry making encompasses many varied disciplines. Although it is not possible to present in this volume all possible techniques in great depth, we hope to establish a solid technical base on which the reader can begin and improve his or her technique. This philosophy is perfectly reflected in the words of Benvenuto Cellini, expressed in his work entitled *"I trattati dell oreficeria e della scultura"*:

"It should not surprise the reader that we have spoken of so many things in this book. I have not even covered half of what I could explain about an art capable of absorbing all of the energies of a man and that requires an entire lifetime fully dedicated to its cultivation."

Related Techniques

Chasing and Repoussé

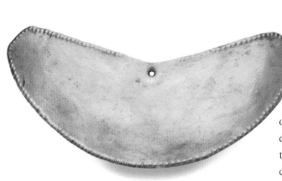
▼ PreColumbian gold pectoral from the Sinú region, 900 A.D.

Pitch

Pitch is the material used to firmly secure the piece for working. It should have a consistency that allows the metal to bend, so that it can be slowly shaped to the desired form by successive hammer blows. Although there are numerous formulas for making pitch, suitable for a great variety of uses, it is essentially composed of a sticky, elastic substance (rosin or pine pitch), a filler to control the degree of stiffness (powdered clay), and an emollient to soften it (oil or tallow).

The techniques of *chasing* and *repoussé* are very important in jewelry making, and have been in existence for centuries. Indeed, they are considered to be a separate craft altogether, and are so intertwined that it is difficult to treat them separately. To speak of one is almost invariably to speak of the other, although technically, repoussé is the art of creating relief from the back, while chasing is used to further decorate a repoussé relief from the front.

Repoussé gives volume or form to a metal sheet. Pitch is a material that is hard and resilient, but with enough elasticity to give beneath the blows of the hammer and chasing tool.

▲ Pitch bowl, pitch, and chasing tools

Preparing the Pitch

Careful pitch preparation yields the best results. Break up the rosin into small pieces, melt it slowly in a pot, and then add the clay, little by little. Stir the mixture constantly to avoid lumping, and do not let it boil. Once the clay and rosin are well mixed, add the oil or tallow, and continue stirring until the mixture is smooth. Pour the pitch into an iron bowl or a wooden box, whichever is most suitable for the work.

It is important to know how to modify the characteristics of the pitch, since its consistency depends on its temperature, and the climate of the region. The requirements of the piece, too, must be taken into consideration. For a softer pitch, add more oil; to harden it, add more clay. Use a softer pitch for creating volume (repoussé) and a harder pitch for modeling and decorative work (chasing).

Formula for a semi-hard pitch:
1 kg rosin + 2 kg red clay + 100 cc olive oil
Another widely used formula is:
2 kg pine pitch + 2 kg red clay + 100 g tallow + 50 g Venice turpentine
Using this formula, the pitch may be softened by adding more tallow or turpentine.

▼ Brooch made of gold, silver, and nickel silver by Carmen Amador

➤ Ingredients for making pitch

The Tools

There are basically three tools: a *chasing hammer*, known for its large, flat face and oval-shaped handle, a *pitch bowl*, and *chasing tools*, also called punches.

▲▼ The pitch bowl is an iron hemisphere that usually has a transversal bar soldered inside, so that when lead is poured inside, to give it weight, the pitch will not come loose as a result of hammering.

▲ The pitch bowl is put on a wooden tri-angular base or a belt of thick leather, so the bowl can be moved and lifted during chasing.

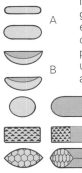

▼ Chasing tools or punches have many forms and functions. There are a) tracing punches, that have blunt, round-cornered working ends used to delineate an outline in the form of a narrow groove; b) embossing punches that are round and used to create volume; c) modeling punches that are flat and used to refine relief forms; and d) matting or graining punches of different shapes and textures, used to create different backgrounds and finishes.

A
B
C
D

Tempering and Making a Chasing Tool

Chasing tools, like many tools used by jewelers, can be made from rods of carbon tool steel. Once cut and prepared, they should be *tempered*; that is, hardened to increase their durability, so that the steel is more resistant to wear and tear. Tempering the steel is essential, not only for the fabrication of chasing tools, but also for many other workshop tools.

Heat the steel until it turns cherry red, but not orange. Quench it immediately, either in oil, or water that contains salt. Oil will give it a softer temper than water, which is important for a very hard steel, such as type f-9 (the higher the number, the harder the steel), which requires a softer temper, or vice versa.

Once tempered, the chasing tool is usually very brittle, and so must be reheated in a controlled manner, then quenched to eliminate the tension produced by the tempering.

The chasing tool must be polished before heating it, so that the color of the metal in the fire can be clearly seen. Apply heat to the first 3 cm of the point until it turns blue, then quench it. This process is detailed in the step-by-step project Repoussé Pendant (page 134), showing the entire process from the beginning drawing to the finished construction.

▲ 1. Cut a piece of type f-5 steel (or f-114—numbering systems can vary with the manufacturer) to a length of about 11 cm. The steel is soft and workable before tempering.

▲ 2. Heat the steel to a cherry red color and, immediately, while still hot, forge it with a hammer. In this case, the point is flattened a little to make a tracer punch.

◄ 3. The steel is now cooled. Shape the tool to the desired form, using a file or a bench grinder and the appropriate sanding sticks.

◄ 4. File and sand the other end of the chasing tool as well, as shown in the photo, so that hammer blows will be distributed evenly on the tool. This photo shows a chasing tool that is ready to be tempered.

➤ 5. The result is a chasing tool with a hardness suited to its function.

Urushi (Japanese Lacquer)

For centuries, it was impossible to know the secrets of *urushi*. They were passed down from father to son in small artisan workshops. The technique originated in China, appearing first as an art form during the Han Dynasty (202 B.C.–220 A.D.), and evolving during the period of the Tang Dynasty. From there it was introduced in Japan, where the technique was perfected. The first lacquered Japanese objects date from the Nara period, when the city served as the country's first permanent capital (710–784 A.D.). Notable development of the technique of urushi occurred during the Heian period (794–1185 A.D.). It reached its splendor at the end of the 16th century and the beginnings of the 17th, during the Azuchi-Momoyama period (1573–1603).

➤ Artist Joaquim Capdevilla applied eggshells to this lacquered piece.

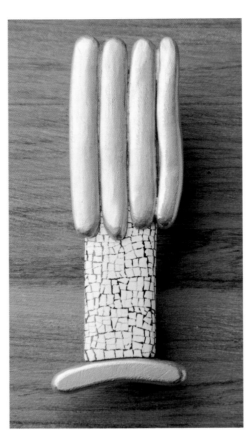

◀ Lacquer in its pure state

▼ Apply lacquer in very fine layers with a brush, sanding each layer after it dries. The brush may be synthetic, but the original brushes used in urushi were made of human hair. Clean them with gasoline or alcohol.

The Lacquers

The technique of urushi consists of the application of various layers of lacquer, most commonly on wood or metal. These lacquers come from the natural resin of the urushi tree, and possess some interesting and advantageous characteristics for jewelry making. They are impervious to humidity and other climactic conditions, as well as to infestation by wood-eating insects. Furthermore, they are durable, and relatively elastic, which allows for the addition of a wide range of pigments and color effects.

Types of Lacquer

Lacquers can be applied in their pure state, or diluted. Each one has its specific application requirements, described in detail in the following section.

For a base lacquer, use *ki-urushi*, although *sesime, nama-urushi, sukinaka nuri,* and *isebaya*, are also used. Isebaya is also used as a final gloss coat. For golden tones and gold leaf, use the lacquer *togidashi nashiji*, and for pigments, use *aka roiro* or *suai*, which produces a darker tone.

For a black lacquer, use *hon kuro*, which is bright and transparent, and *kuro roiro*, which is darker and must be mixed with black pigment. For the technique using eggshells use sukinaka nuri, and for glossy finishes, the isebaya gloss lacquer.

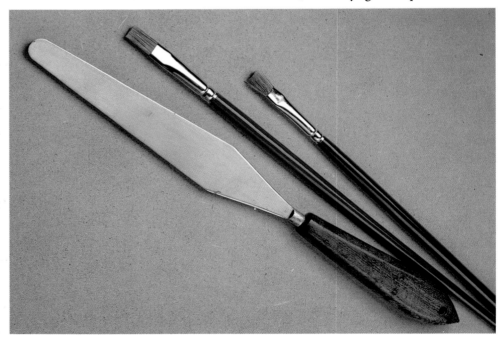

Preparing the Colors

Use lacquer in its undiluted form to prepare a base surface, to apply a gloss, or to obtain relief surfaces. When adding a pigment, however, dilute the lacquer first, and then add the pigment, as described in the following steps:

◄ 1. Dissolve camphor in alcohol until the alcohol evaporates, and a fine white camphor powder remains. Mix this powder with the lacquer, until it has a consistency slightly lighter than that of honey, which could take a concentration of up to as much as 50%.

▼ 2. To create the color, add an organic powdered pigment to the mixture. Here a red pigment is used.

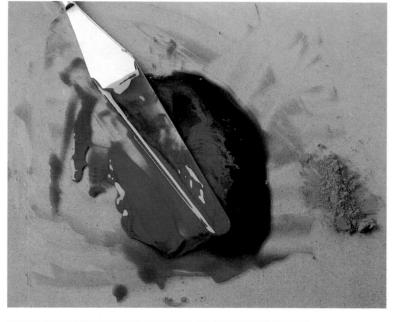

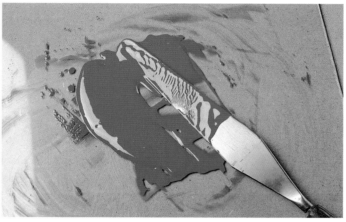

▲ 3. The lacquer shows its true color only at the end of the process, when it is dry; it takes some experience in mixing to prepare exactly the right color.

▼ Variations of a lacquered necklace by Estela Guitart

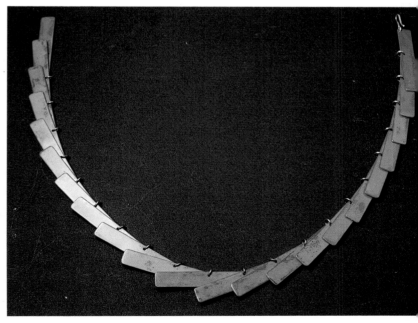

◀ Bracelet with lacquered gold leaf by Estela Guitart

Application Process

Lacquer can be applied to a variety of surfaces: wood (with the exception of olive wood), leather, ceramic, and metal. The only condition is that the surface must be very clean. Sand it with a medium-grade sandpaper, and use *trichlorethylene* to eliminate any oils.

Possible Applications

The following section demonstrates a series of different applications of Japanese lacquer. In all of them, use the base lacquer ki-urushi, with the exception of the technique that uses eggshells, which uses suki-naka nuri. When the first coat of base lacquer is dry, sand it with a very fine grade of wet/dry sandpaper and then begin applying subsequent coats.

➤ An aluminum sheet in which two layers of ki-urushi have been applied. This base lacquer provides the base for the colored lacquers that follow. If the base coat is not applied, the colors will all turn an intense black.

Lacquering consists of four phases. The first is to apply the base lacquer on the selected surface. Once the base coat is dry, sand, and check that the lacquer covers the entire surface. If not, apply another coat of base lacquer.

After applying the base lacquer, apply a lacquer mixed with pigment, using one of the techniques that follow in this section. Since lacquering consists of applying successive coats with a brush, each coat must dry in an atmosphere having a minimum humidity of 60%. Put the piece in a small humidor for at least a full day. A faster method, however, is to put the piece in an electric kiln for about three hours at a temperature of 100–150°C.

Sand each coat of lacquer with wet/dry sandpaper so that the surface is even, eliminating residue that could prevent the next layer from adhering properly. Only fine to very-fine grades of sandpaper are used in this process. Use 800-grit for sanding the most pronounced irregularities. Use the highest grade on the very last coat to make the surface as smooth as possible.

Finally, apply a coat of isebaya gloss lacquer, using a folded cloth. Let it dry in the open air for 20 minutes until it is absorbed. Eliminate any excess lacquer with a silk cloth, and let it dry in an electric kiln for about three hours at 100–150°C. Some lacquers, such as suai, nashiji, or hon kuro, don't necessarily shine when used as a last layer.

After applying the gloss lacquer it is ready for the final finish. First, apply the polishing compound *kagayaki*, until it is completely absorbed into the piece. Then do the same with the buffing compound called *migaki* 5,000.

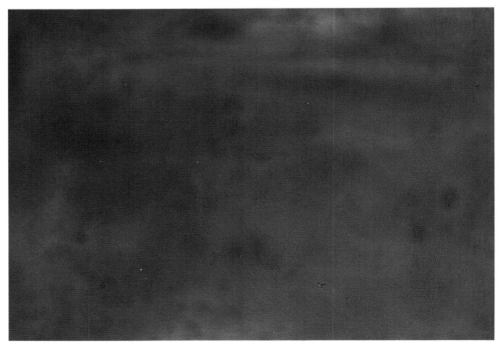

Application #1

To achieve the effect shown here, first apply a coat of aka roiro with red pigment on the base lacquer. Then, place grains of rice on the surface and let the piece dry for 20 minutes in a kiln. Remove it from the kiln and carefully remove the rice grains, as the lacquer is still not completely dry. Take off all the rice, and put the piece back in the kiln to finish drying. Don't sand the piece yet, or the relief created by the rice will be removed. Next, apply several coats of kuro roiro with black pigment. Sand the first layer of kuro roiro gently, but don't sand down the relief too much. After each coat, sand a little more until the relief left by the rice in the red lacquer is evened out, and has a completely smooth surface. Finally, apply a coat of hon kuro diluted with camphor. This gloss lacquer gives the piece a gleaming finish when used as the final coat, but sand it with a 2,000-grit sandpaper to remove any impurities. Finally, polish and buff the piece to a high shine.

▼ Application #1

Application #2

Apply a coat of diluted hon kuro. Place grains of rice on the surface and let it dry for 20 minutes in a kiln, then remove the rice. Return it to the kiln to finish drying, but don't sand it. Next, put on a coat of aka roiro mixed with green pigment, then dry and sand. Apply another coat of the same lacquer, but with a higher concentration of pigment than the first layer. Sand the surface completely. Apply the isebaya gloss lacquer, and finish by polishing and buffing.

▲ Application # 2

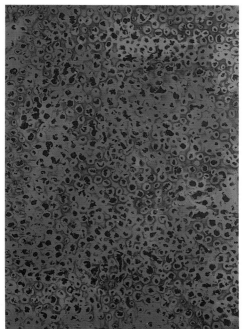

Application #3

First prepare aka roiro with blue pigment. Then, as in the first two examples, place rice grains on the surface (different-sized grains produce different effects), put the piece in the kiln for 20 minutes, remove the rice, and put the piece back in the kiln to finish drying. Do not sand. Next, apply two different coats of aka roiro, the first with blue pigments and the second with green, until the relief left by the rice is even, and the last coat is perfectly smooth. As in the previous examples, sand between each coat before proceeding to the next one. Coat it with isebaya gloss lacquer, and once dry, proceed with the final finish by polishing and buffing.

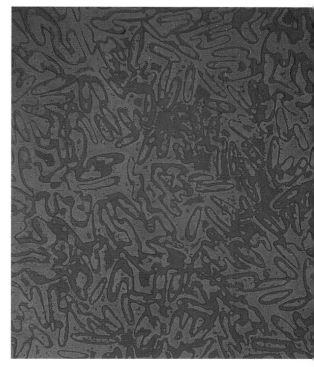

▲ Application # 3

Application #4

The first coat is aka roiro with red pigment. This time, place small round pasta on the surface, and put it in the kiln to dry for 20 minutes. Take off the pasta, and finish drying the piece in the kiln. Do not sand. Next, apply various coats of suai, sanding between each layer with a 2,000-grit sandpaper, then polish and buff the piece.

◄ Application # 4

Application #5

In this application, use aka roiro with a dark green pigment, and again place small round pasta on the surface; put the piece in the to dry. Take off the pasta, return it to the kiln; do not sand. Then, apply several coats of aka roiro with various shades of green pigments, until the surface is smooth. Sand between each application. Use the isebaya gloss lacquer, and finish with polishing and buffing.

Application #6

Use the lacquer aka roiro with a terracotta pigment, and put on one coat. Place different pasta of various shapes on the surface, and dry in the kiln as before. Remove the pasta, replace it in the kiln to dry completely, and don't sand. Apply various coats of aka roiro, using white pigment; vary the quantity of pigment with each coat until, with successive sandings, the final smooth layer is obtained. Proceed with isebaya gloss lacquer, then polish and buff.

▼ Application # 6

▼Application # 5

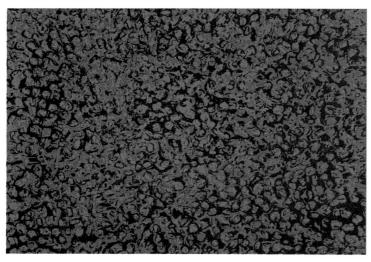

Application #7

Use the lacquer hon kuro in its undiluted state. On top of this, place long pasta, dry for 20 minutes in a kiln, remove the pasta, and put the piece back in the kiln. Do not sand. In this example, we have applied different layers of aka roiro with shades of green to one-half of the piece, and on the other half, aka roiro with shades of blue. Use isebaya gloss lacquer as a gloss coat, and finish by polishing and buffing.

Application #8

Apply kuro roiro with black pigment in an irregular fashion, to create relief. Let this dry, but do not sand. Apply a coat of aka roiro with white pigment, and sand after it dries. Apply several coats of dissolved suai, until the surface is smooth. Finish with sanding, using 2,000-grit sandpaper, polishing, and buffing.

▼ Application # 7

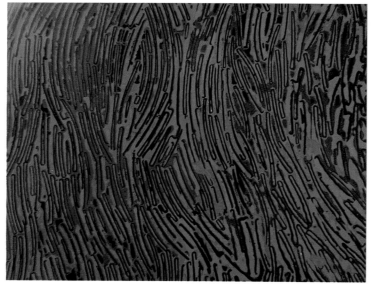

▼ Application # 8

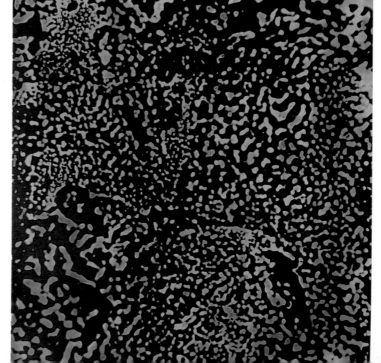

Application #9

Apply a very thick coat of undiluted ki-urushi, so that it contracts and forms a wrinkled surface. Let it dry in a kiln; do not sand.

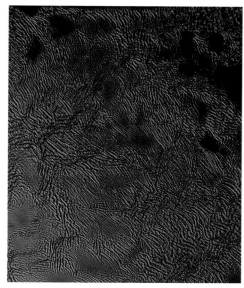

▲ Application # 9

Application #12

On a surface of togidashi nashiji, place a layer of gold leaf, and let it dry in a kiln for at least three hours. Do not sand. Apply another coat of togidashi nashiji, and let it dry, then sand with 2,000-grit sandpaper, and polish and buff.

▼ Application # 12

Application #10

Apply undiluted hon kuro thickly so that it forms a relief surface. Let it dry and don't sand. Apply successive coats of aka roiro with red pigment, until the surface is smooth, sanding between coats. Finally, apply diluted suai, and finish sanding, with 2,000-grit sandpaper, then polish and buff.

▲ Application #10

Application #13

In this technique, start with the base lacquer sukinaka nuri, and sand. On this, apply a coat of undiluted sukinaka nuri. While this is still slightly wet, place small pieces of eggshell, so that they fit together like a puzzle on the surface. Remove the interior membrane from the eggshell first, and very carefully place the pieces so that the concave surfaces face up. Use a little bit of epoxy if needed, but don't let it seep out between the pieces. Next, apply several layers of undiluted sukinaka nuri, until the spaces between the eggshells are filled, and the last layer is perfectly smooth. Since, in this case, the lacquer is used as a filler, do not sand between layers. Sand only the last coat. The eggshells will discolor slightly upon the first application of sukinaka nuri. For white eggshells, continue sanding the piece, to eliminate the remaining lacquer.

Application #11

For this effect, apply a coat of diluted togidashi nashiji. Next, sprinkle a very fine powdered aluminum on the lacquer, and dry it in the kiln; don't sand. Apply another coat of diluted togidashi nashiji, and sand. Repeat this process, alternating sprinkling aluminum powder with every other coat. Do not use aluminum powder in the last coat. Sand, polish, and buff.

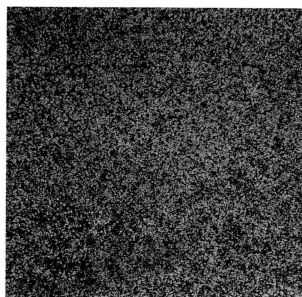

▲ Application #11

▼ Application #13

Making a Bracelet

This project is a bracelet made of linked metal sheets that are slightly concave. The entire process is illustrated, from the application of the base coat to the final polishing.

➤ 1. First, sand the pieces, and then clean them with trichlorethylene; try to keep them from any contact with dust or oils from the skin.

▼ 2. Carefully apply a thin, uniform coat of base lacquer, in this case ki-urushi.

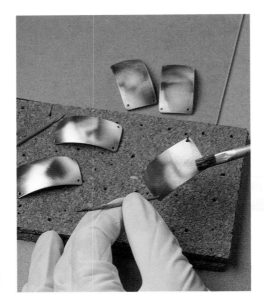

◄ 3. Next, start the drying process. If a humidor or an appropriate kiln is not in the workshop, use an ordinary kitchen kiln, as shown here.

➤ 4. When the plates are dry, sand them with a fine sandpaper, and check that the base lacquer completely covers the surface.

▲ 5. Apply a coat of kuro roiro mixed with black pigment and, once dry, sand the surface, so that it is perfectly smooth.

◄ 6. Next, apply another coat of kuro roiro with black pigment. This is the layer for using the pasta.

➤ 7. Carefully place the pasta on the surface with tweezers, keeping the composition in mind.

▲ 8. After the pieces have been in the kiln for 20 minutes, remove the pasta, and place the pieces back in the kiln to finish drying.

▲ 9. Without sanding the pieces, apply a coat of aka roiro with red pigment. Place the pieces in the kiln to dry, and the pigment will create the effect shown in this photo.

▲ 10. Sand the pieces until the pattern of the lacquer underneath appears on the surface.

▲ 11. Once sanded and clean, apply the polish, then buff, using isebaya gloss lacquer as the buffing compound, which will give the pieces a better shine.

▲ 12. On the underside of the plates, apply gold leaf on the lacquer.

➤ 13. The interior of the bracelet is shown in this photo. Note the detail of the closure.

▲ 14. The pieces of the bracelet are linked together with silver jump rings.

➤ Bracelet by Estela Guitart

Enameling

Enameling brings to jewelry making the possibility of color in all its chromatic brilliance. Originating from the application and interrelationship of two basic elements, glass and fire, enameling offers a wide variety of color choices to the jeweler. The enameling processes presented in this section do not require complicated equipment. Only a small kiln (capable of reaching 900°C), a variety of well-made brushes, and a small mortar and pestle for grinding the enamel, are needed.

Enamels

Enamel is an overglaze material composed principally of silicates, borates, aluminates, and different oxides: copper, manganese, and iron, that give the enamel its color. Enamel can be applied in different forms: as an oil-based paste, as a wet powder, or as a dry powder. The paste form, called *overglaze enamel*, gives an effect very much like that of oil paint. Different types of enamels also exist: opaque, translucent, and opalescent. There is also a special enamel flux, which is not to be confused with the flux ordinarily used in jewelry making.

◄ This enamel work by Miquel Soldevila is a portrait of his friend, Francesc Cambó. The story has it that Cambó refused the piece, saying that Soldevila had captured his soul.

▼ This photo shows opaque enamel in its original form and in powder form. This enamel contains its own color and brilliance and doesn't permit light to pass through it.

◄ This piece, featuring opalescent enamel, is from the collection of Lluís Masriera. This type of enamel has a milky quality that allows light to pass through it. Its color will vary, depending on the underlying surface tone.

▼ Transparent enamel allows light to pass through it; its shine depends on the underlying surface.

Washing the Enamel

Enamel in powder form may be purchased from a commercial supplier, but it needs to be washed and ground a bit more before using it. Adding a little bit of water, grind the enamel with a mortar and pestle, as described in the steps below.

➤ 1. Place the enamel powder in the mortar, and add a little water. Grind it using circular motions, to make a finer powder. This will result in a rather thick, cloudy solution that should be rinsed with more water. Don't grind large quantities of enamel at one time.

▲ 2. Put the contents of the mortar into a tall glass. Fill the glass with water, and stir. Let it sit until the enamel settles, then pour off the water. Repeat this operation seven times. After the final rinse, add five drops of nitric acid, and let it react on the enamel for one minute. Add more water, and stir with a clean glass rod. Repeat the rinsing procedure six more times.

◄ 3. The process of adding water, stirring, and settling should be repeated about 12 times altogether. Use distilled water in the last few rinses.

◄ 4. After the final six rinses, the enamel should appear as shown in the photo. After you pour off the last rinse, keep the wet enamel in a closed, transparent jar.

▼ Before beginning to enamel, it is a good idea to make a color palette, like the one shown here. Enamel takes on its true color only after it is fired, and the tone will vary, depending on the number of coats applied, and the tone of the base surface used.

Application

Transparent and opalescent enamels are affected by their underlying surfaces. The same enamel will look different, depending upon whether it is applied to gold, silver, or copper. The same is true when applying transparent and opalescent enamel over another color. In general, enamel can be applied on gold, silver, and copper, but never brass. The metal should be annealed and free of oxides and oils before beginning to enamel. Transparent enamel can be applied on *gold* or *silver leaf*, heightening the color of the metal, and producing a different effect.

It's best to apply enamel in thin, uniform layers, rather than in thick coats. This method offers better control over the color, and prevents the enamel from cracking.

Enamel is a delicate material and should be worked with carefully, away from the dust and dirt of the workshop, and especially the buffing machine. The slightest speck of dust will be seen in the final result.

Counterenamel and Flux

To counteract the tensions formed in metal when it is subjected to heat, first apply a *counterenamel* on the reverse side of the piece. This should be done with all sheet metal except very thick pieces. When using transparent enamels especially, apply a coat of flux to the front side. Once fired, you can apply the colored enamel on top and fire it in turn.

➤ 1. Apply enamel on flat or slightly curved surfaces. To curve a flat surface, form the sheet with a wooden embossing punch on a soft surface such as a telephone book.

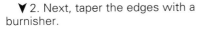
▼ 2. Next, taper the edges with a burnisher.

◀ 3. Before applying the counterenamel, cover the surface with diluted gum arabic so that the counterenamel will adhere better.

➤ 4. Sprinkle the counterenamel evenly on the surface, using a sieve.

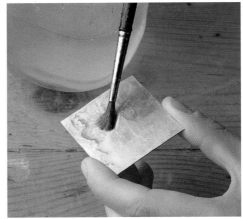

▲ 5. Enamel flux is a transparent, colorless enamel applied directly to the clean, metal surface. Apply a heavy, thick layer, as shown in the photo, and fire it in a kiln.

▲ 6. This photo shows two different sheets prepared with flux and counterenamel, ready to be enameled. Counterenamel is always applied first, then the flux.

➤ 7. Holding it vertically, load the brush with enamel and deposit it onto the metal plate. Overglaze enamel—unlike other kinds of enamels—retains the expressive quality of brushstrokes, as in painting.

Firing

Firing enamel in the kiln brings out the color and sets the finish. There are hard enamels that fire at high temperatures of 950°C, and others that are softer and need temperatures of 750–825°C, depending on the enamel manufacturer. For most firing purposes, use 900°C and increase or decrease the time that the enamel stays in the kiln, depending on the type and color. Other factors that influence the firing time are the hardness of the enamel, the thickness of the piece, and its size. Once it is fired, remove the piece from the kiln and let it cool before handling.

◄ 1. Before putting the enamel in the kiln, dry it by placing it under an infrared light, such as shown here. Alternately, move the piece in and out of an open kiln; this will keep the water contained in the enamel from boiling.

▼ 2. Put the enamel in the kiln using an iron trivet or any small sheet of refractory material as a base.

Overglaze Enamel

Overglaze enamels are prepared by placing a little powdered enamel on a sheet of glass and adding lavender oil or liquefied petroleum jelly. Mix with a spatula until the mixture has the consistency of oil paint. Apply overglaze enamels on a base of white, opaque enamel. Firing time is usually a little less than that of powdered enamel.

▲ This brooch by Ramón Puig is highlighted with overglaze enamel work by Francesca Ribes.

◄ Different colors of overglaze enamel have varying degrees of consistency on this palette.

➤ Fire overglaze enamels last, using a lower firing temperature. This keeps their soft colors intact.

Cloisonné

Cloisonné was first practiced in ancient Egypt and Mesopotamia as a substitute for using precious stones. The Byzantines, however, became the great masters of the art. The process consists of dividing a surface into small spaces or cells using gold, silver, or copper wire, and filling the spaces with enamel.

Some jewelers use gold solder to solder the wire cells in place. The most common and practical method, however, uses enamel flux. First, draw or etch your design on the piece and then coat it with a layer of enamel flux. Fire the piece and then lay the wire on top, after shaping it with pliers. To hold the wire in place on the flux, apply a bit of *gum tragacanth*.

Once all the wires are in place, fire it. Then, begin to fill all the cells with color, firing with each application. Finishing this, stone the enamel down with a *carborundum stone*, and fire it one more time to even out the enamel and set the final finish.

▲ Many times cloisonné and champlevé are used in the same piece. Here, cloisonné was used for the detailed, precision work. Master Eibertus, ceiling piece representing the ascension of Christ. Kunstgewerbemuseum, Berlin.

➤ Grisalle is a painted enamel generally used to represent human figures and ornamental motifs.

Grisaille

Grisaille is usually worked on a dark surface with layers of Limoges-like, opaque white underpainting, or a very finely ground opalescent enamel. When fired, the white sinks into the black, melting and creating shadows and highlights in tones of gray. Successive coats, fired one after another, reveal the design. The thicker the coats, the stronger the white highlights will be.

Plique-à-jour

In *plique-à-jour*, the enamel is held in place by the walls of cutout spaces. With successive applications and firing, it fills the cutouts and gives the appearance of stained glass. Since no underlying surface is used, light passes all the way through the enamel.

▼ 1. Before beginning, apply gum arabic to the interior of the cutout. For the technique of plique-à-jour, use a paintbrush or spatula to apply the enamel to the inside of a cutout shape. Several applications will be necessary to fill the cutout completely.

◄ Pendant made with plique-à-jour. Lluís Masriera collection

➤ 2. Once the cutout is filled, stone the piece with a carborundum stone to eliminate all the leftover enamel. Fire it one last time to even out the enamel and give it a final finish.

Champlevé

This is a technique used by the Persians, Greeks, Romans, and the nomadic tribes of the Asiatic steppes, who transmitted the craft to the Celts and other European peoples. During the Romantic period, a great quantity of religious work was created using this art form.

Champlevé uses enamel to fill lines made on a metal surface etched with acid or with a graver or chisel. Fire and stone it with a carborundum stone until the enamel lies even with the metal surface. Fire it a final time for a finished surface.

In the kiln the enamel shrinks into a concave shape, making it necessary to apply several coats until the enamel is higher than the surface of the metal. *Stoning* cleans the excess enamel off the surface so that it can be fired one last time for a finish.

▲ Champlevé bracelet by Aureli Bisbe

➤ One variation of champlevé, basse-taille, consists of applying translucent enamel on a gold or silver surface that has been hammered or acid-etched to give it volume.

➤ Enamel applied over relief. Lluís Masriera collection

Enameled Brooch

Deciding on the color, design, and execution of an enameled piece takes careful planning.

Here we demonstrate creating some simple but very charming brooches using the technique of champlevé.

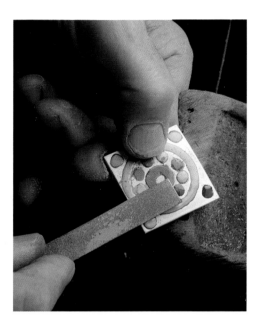

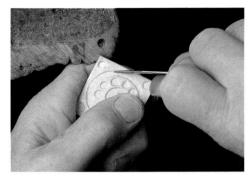

▲1. With a graver, etch the design where the enamel will be applied.

➤ 2. Paint on the enamel with a brush, taking care to wash the brush well after each change of color.

◄ 3. After the enamel fires in the kiln at 900°C, file the surface with a diamond file.

➤ Champlevé brooches by Aureli Bisbe

Niello

Niello is not really an enamel, but its form of application is so similar that it has been historically linked with enameling techniques. It was used by the Minoan and Mycaean cultures and in Renaissance Europe. Examples of this technique are common in religious artifacts dating from 300–700 A.D.

Niello continues to be used in India and in Islamic countries. Many jewelers are today returning to the technique of niello in their work. As a decorative material, it has the advantage of being easy to prepare and apply. Moreover, it doesn't require a kiln or any special ingredients.

Proportions used in niello			
Silver	Copper	Lead	Sulfur
1	2	3	6
1	1	2	8
1	2	4	5

▲Detail of the chalice of Tassilo with applied niello. Treasure of the Kremsmünster Monastery

The Composition of Niello

Niello is an alloy made of silver, copper, lead, and sulfur. Its gray color provides a striking contrast when applied on gold or silver. It also has the advantage of melting at a low temperature, so that its application is not too complicated.

Preparation

Niello is created when sulfur is added to the three metals of the alloy. First, melt the silver, copper, and lead together with borax in a crucible that is only used for the preparation of niello. Once they melt, add an abundant amount of sulfur and a little ammonium chloride. Working in a well-ventilated space, and wearing a respirator, stir the mixture with a wooden rod. Once it stops smoking, pour the paste-like liquid into a mold and let it cool. Grind the molded metal into a powder, add a little more sulfur, and re-melt it.

Grind the niello a second time into a very fine powder using an old mortar and pestle, preferably one of iron. Dampen the powder slightly by adding a little gum arabic diluted in water.

Niello is ideal for applying to surfaces that have been etched, so long as the depth is no greater than 1 millimeter.

◀ Ground niello

Application

The surface of the metal should be pickled and clean of oils. Wet the surface with flux and apply the niello with a brush. Let it dry; then place it on a metal trivet or a thin sheet of iron and melt it in a kiln or with a torch, making sure the flame doesn't directly touch the niello. Avoid excessive temperatures that could make the niello porous.

After it has cooled, eliminate excess niello with a file and appropriate emery papers until the surface is level and the surrounding metal is uncovered.

▲ 1. Make an etching on which to apply the niello. Use either a brush or a metal spatula. Apply niello the same way you apply for enamel, so that it overflows the surface.

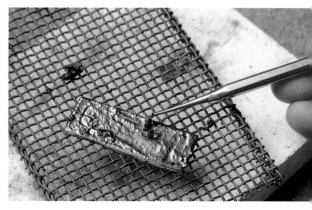

▲ 2. Apply indirect heat. Spread the niello with a spatula so that it penetrates the entire surface.

◀ 3. Once cool, file the piece with an old file, then sand the surface smooth.

Safety Measures

Niello contains lead, so be very careful to prevent the filings and scraps from contaminating other metals. Always file niello away from the work bench, and discard the crucibles and emery papers that have come into contact with it. Melt the metal in a well-ventilated place to avoid breathing the fumes, because they are highly toxic.

➤ Niello applied unevenly over a relatively smooth surface. Piece by Carles Codina

STONE SETTING

Setting a stone for display is often the only reason for the construction of a piece of jewelry. Stone setting has always been integral to jewelry making, and the specialized technique of stone setting came from this desire to show stones off to their best advantage; nowadays, however, it is such a specialized occupation that it is virtually a separate craft in and of itself. In fact, orthodox settings often dominate the initial concept of the design, at the expense of the design itself, and in this way stone setting has become disconnected from the art of jewelry making as a whole. A solid understanding of how to make settings and correctly set stones confers more freedom in the creation of jewelry, and allows greater flexibility to integrate the setting into the larger conceptual design.

Tools

The equipment necessary for stone setting is relatively inexpensive and easy to prepare. The process requires gravers of different shapes and sizes, an alcohol lamp, dopping wax, dopping sticks for holding the piece in place, a bench grinder, and good lighting.

◄ An example of an unorthodox setting. *Ship with Caged Lovers*, Germany, 1570, Museo Degli Argenti, Florence

▲ Brooch with various types of stones and settings by Ramón Puig Cuyàs

➤ Some basic stone setting equipment: various gravers, a bezel pusher with its characteristic round handle, and a waxstick, which is indispensable for handling the stones.

Gravers

Gravers are the most common of all the stone setting tools. A *graver* is a steel tool that, when properly prepared, is used to cut metal, make adjustments to settings, raise beads, and decorate or trim metal. Begin with a flat graver, a round graver, and an *onglette* graver.

▼This drawing shows the proper angle and amount of metal to remove from the original form of the graver so that it will have the correct shape for stone setting.

➤ 1. Here, gravers are shown before and after shaping. Snap off the point so that the graver's length fits your hand comfortably, then bevel it to the shape and angle shown below.

▼ 2. In order not to overheat the point of the graver while grinding, keep dipping the end in water. Otherwise, the heat will anneal the point, and the graver will lose the temper it needs to cut well.

▼ 3. Continue dipping the graver end in water while filing the angle so that it doesn't overheat.

▲ 4. After getting the proper cut and angle on the graver, file the bevel by rubbing it on an Arkansas stone treated with a little oil. Do this regularly as you use the tool to keep it in good condition.

Bezel Pusher

This tool is easy to make, and is indispensable both for pressing the metal prongs onto the stone, and for closing the setting, which keeps the stone in place. Make the *bezel pusher* by annealing the point of an old file handle, then filing it with another file or with a bench grinder, giving it one of the shapes shown in the photo to the right. On the other end, attach a round, wooden handle.

In order to keep the bezel pusher from slipping while closing a setting, give the point a rough texture by hitting it with an old file so that the texture of the file is imprinted onto the point.

▲Bezel and prong pushers, shaped according to the needs and habits of the jeweler

Dopping Wax and Dopping Sticks

Stone settings should be firmly fixed in a rigid substance called *dopping wax*. The wax, in turn, needs to be applied to a support called a *dopping stick*. Dopping sticks may be shaped with a lengthwise split for holding rings, or in any form that is convenient for holding flatter pieces, such as brooches or pendants.

Dopping wax is made of red flake shellac, yellow ocher, and rosin. The proportion of these ingredients may vary, according to climate and custom. The most common proportion is to mix equal parts of all three. Although this wax bears a resemblance to chasing pitch and is prepared in the same way, it is much stronger and has an entirely different function.

Motorized Hand Tools

You will need burs of various shapes and sizes. Spherical and concave burs are recommended to round beads and prongs. Although a flex shaft motor (which transmits the rotation to the interchangeable handpiece by way of a flexible shaft) can be conveniently hung out of the way, the micro motor is even more convenient because the motor is contained in the handpiece itself, making it more versatile and comfortable to use. Both types of motors, however, can be used in stone setting.

▲ The flex shaft has a motor that is separate from the handpiece, and the power is transmitted through a flexible shaft. Both the micro motor and the flex shaft perform the same functions and both accommodate attachments such as the hammer handpiece, which has different tips for closing prongs. A selection of various shapes and sizes of burs, especially round shapes, is essential for removing metal and making adjustments in settings.

▲ Slowly melt the ingredients together in a pot, but don't boil them. Pour the contents onto a wet steel sheet, and let cool. Once cooled, you can break up the wax into smaller pieces with a hammer.

▼ To soften the dopping wax and fix the setting to it, warm it with the flame from an alcohol lamp. Apply a liberal coat of oil to the setting first so that you can easily remove it from the wax when the work is finished. To remove any pieces of wax stuck to the setting, boil the piece in diluted ammonia.

Setter's Waxstick

Stone setting involves continual handling and adjustment of small stones for a good fit. To facilitate this handling, stone setters have special tools. Presented here is a kind of stone holder that is very easy to make, using an old bur, a little soft wax, and a stick of drawing charcoal.

➤ 1. With a mortar and pestle, grind the charcoal to a fine powder. Anneal both ends of an old bur, then flatten them with a hammer.

▼ 2. Mix the charcoal powder with the wax until it has the consistency of clay, and form this clay around the bur in the shape of a small pear ending in a point. (Coat the bur with lacquer first, to keep the clay from simply revolving around it.)

▼ 3. When finished, the tool should be sticky enough to adhere to the table of a stone, as shown in the photo.

Types of Settings and Stone Setting Methods

A *setting* is the metal support for holding the stone. The fabrication of a setting is intrinsically linked to how the stone will be set.

There are many ways to set a stone, and many different types of settings possible. In this section, we look at a few of the basic concepts of stone setting. These basics will establish a foundation for creative work in the future.

Before beginning the construction of a setting, it is very important to examine the stone carefully, noting its physical properties and size. Use a *vernier caliper* to precisely measure it.

▲ In these settings by Joan Aviñó, stones are set table-to-table.

▲ For maximum color and brilliance, stones are cut in mathematically exact planes called facets. The final result is known as the stone's "cut". Here are shown some of the different diamond cuts.

➤ The basic purpose of any setting is to prevent the stone from moving either horizontally or vertically. The seat controls horizontal and downward movement, while metal pressed on top of the stone limits vertical and upward movement.

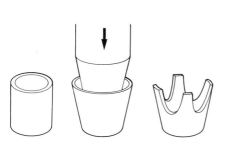

◄ This stone setting by Carles Codina was prepared by polishing the interior of a half-tube shaped metal sheet to highlight the brilliance of the stone, and using various types of prongs, including the foot of the angel.

Tube Setting

The most simple settings are those constructed from a metal tube. For small brilliant-cut stones, the minimum wall thickness is about .6 mm. The inside diameter of the setting must be about one-third smaller than the outer diameter of the stone's *girdle*. This is so that when you carve the *bearing* on which the stone sits, there is a small metal border extending above the girdle that can be folded down over the stone to secure it in place.

A stone with a large *culet* usually requires a setting of greater height and thickness. A fragile stone, such as an emerald, should be set in a softer metal, perhaps 22-karat gold, while more resilient gems, such as diamonds or sapphires, can be set in almost any kind of setting.

▲ This tool is used to flare a bezel into different tube sizes to then use as settings. It is called a bezel-forming punch set and comes in practically every shape and size needed. Insert an annealed metal tube inside one of the holes and hit it gently with the point in order to form a tube setting.

➤ Another possibility, also starting with a tube, is to solder a ring to the base after making the prongs.

▲ Starting with a tube shape and using a bezel-forming punch, hit the tube with the punch to form the setting. It can be used just as it is to set a stone, but often some of the metal can be eliminated with a file; then a bur is used to make from four to six prongs in the setting.

The Process

Stone setting involves leaving a few millimeters of excess metal in the upper portion of the bearing that can be pressed over the stone, to prevent it from falling out. To do this correctly, it is very important to fit the stone into the setting precisely so that there is enough metal left on top to secure it properly.

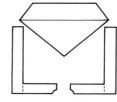

◄▼1 and 2. Using a flat graver and a round graver, begin in the middle of the thickness of the wall and eliminate metal from the interior of the tube so that the stone fits correctly into the tube's interior.

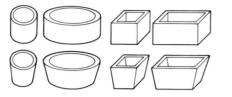

▲ With the proper tools, any shape can be used to form a bezel.

◄ A setting of this kind doesn't always have to be shaped from a tube. Here a rectangular wire of white gold, alloyed with palladium for strength and firmly secured to the body of the ring, is used as a setting.

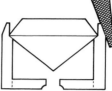

◄ 3. Once the stone is seated, file away a little of the metal on the exterior of the tube at an angle.

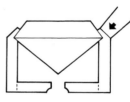

◄ 4. Next, close the opening with a bezel pusher, and use a flex shaft with a hammer handpiece to tighten the setting, as well as to work-harden it.

◄ The setting process in this ring by Carles Codina is the same as that of a metal tube.

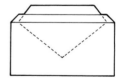

◄5. With a flat graver, shape the interior metal where there is the most contact with the stone, to eliminate any imperfections. Finally, burnish the setting.

Prong Setting

The *prong setting*, also called a *claw setting*, is used frequently, and is one of the settings that covers the least amount of the stone's surface area. In this kind of setting, it is important to ensure that the prongs are strong enough, and are spaced evenly so that the stones cannot come loose.

The Process

Eliminate metal to form the prongs with a ball bur. Use a smaller, ball bur to create the exact size needed in the interior for the stone to fit. Place the stone in the setting and use a bezel pusher to press the wire prongs over the stone. Then, shape the wire with a small file and round it with a concave bur.

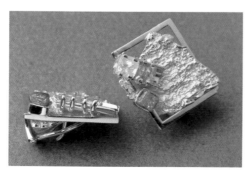

◄ Ring by Daniel Kruger

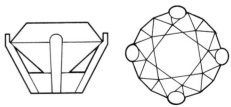

▲Classic setting with prongs. At least four prongs are needed in this type of setting to prevent the stone from moving or falling out. All of the cuts made in the prongs need to be at the same height so that the stone doesn't lean to one side.

◄There are no rules governing the structure of a setting, but the method of securely setting the stones remains constant. Earrings by Carles Codina

Channel Setting

This type of setting is used for placing a series of stones of the same size in a line and is often used in wedding rings. Use stones of a brilliant cut, or any kind of square or rectangular cut—so long as the stones are well calibrated—since the setting will be the same for all of them.

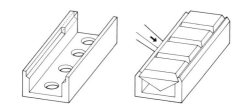

Cabochon Cut Stones

Cabochon is a type of cut in which the stones are cut flat on the bottom and round on the top and need a special kind of setting and setting procedure. This cut is an innovation arising from the Art Nouveau movement, which represented a break with the classically faceted cuts of traditional jewelry, and reflected the modern age. It is used to highlight colors and optical effects, especially in opaque and translucent stones.

The Process

The following photos show the process for setting a cabochon cut stone, including eliminating the metal from the wall and closing the setting.

▲ 2. First, use a round bur to make a bearing so that the flat side of the stone can be seated inside. With different gravers, adjust the seat so that the stone sits level and fits snugly in place with a depth of no more than 1 millimeter.

The Process

The method consists in eliminating metal from the interior of the wall of the channel with a round bur, followed by using gravers, to form a *bearing*. Once the bearing is correctly adjusted, file the exterior edge a little bit to form an angle. Fit the first stone in place and close the metal with a prong pusher until the setting is tight. Repeat this process with the other stones, making sure that their height, and the distance between them, is the same. Once they are in place use a hammer handpiece to tighten them; then file, sand, and polish the walls of the setting so that the finish is uniform.

◄ Drawing of a channel setting

▲ Rings by Pilar Garrigosa with set cabochons

▲ 3. Close the opening with a bezel pusher, as illustrated in the drawings to the right. File the exterior and give it a final finish. Using a flat graver, smooth out any irregularities at the border where the setting is in contact with the stone. Then, even out the surface and give it a final finish with a burnisher.

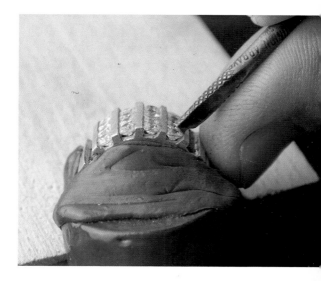

▲ Brilliant-cut diamonds placed in a channel. The process is the same, but the fitting should be adapted to the cut of the stone.

➤ 1. In this example, we are using a rectangular wire that is a little more than 1 millimeter thick. It has been formed slightly with a bezel punch. A flat piece will be soldered underneath as a base and the excess filed smooth to the contour of the setting.

➤ The metal should rest on top of the cabochon and should be tightened with a bezel pusher in the order shown below. Shape the exterior with a file and the interior with a graver.

➤ The correct order for tightening the setting of a cabochon stone. First, press and close the metal at one point, then press and close the metal on precisely the opposite side. Continue closing the setting in this manner, alternating sides until the stone is completely enclosed.

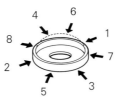

Cabochon Setting

There are different ways to make settings for this cut of stone. In this case, we have made a setting from two rectangular wires of different heights and soldered them together so that they form a ready-made bearing for the stone.

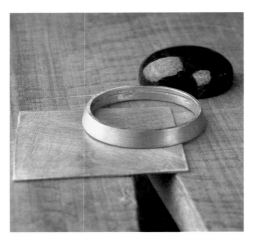

➤ 1. One of the ways to set a cabochon consists of making two rectangular wires. In this case, the wires are of the same thickness, but depending upon the shape of the setting and the stone, the interior wire could be made a little thicker. Solder both wires together with hard solder and mold it to the shape of the stone.

▲ 2. After forming the bezel, solder it to a flat sheet.

◄ 3. File off the excess sheet metal and sand the edge of the sheet flush to the outer edge of the wire.

➤ 4. The setting will eventually be soldered to a rectangular structure that will support the setting, making a pendant.

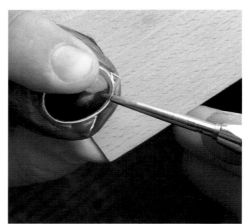

◄ 5. The stone should fit in the seat of the setting just as it is, but it is a good idea to go over it with a graver before closing the opening. Use a bezel pusher to tighten the opening first, and go over it again with the hammer handpiece.

➤ 6. This is the final result.

➤ Here is a variation of a cabochon setting. The teeth were made with a small file.

Another Cabochon Setting

Here, we have made a setting with small balls, like those used in granulation, that have been soldered to the ends of gold wire prongs. The prongs have been soldered to a thicker rectangular wire that serves as the stone's seat.

➤➤ Once the support and the setting are finished, close the prongs, using a smooth prong pusher, without leaving marks on the metal.

Square and Rectangular Stones

It is always important to examine the cut of the stone, as well as its characteristics and dimensions. These types of cuts have many variations that require different settings.

The straight cut, either *baguette* or octagonal, is very common, especially for fragile stones such as emeralds. Each cut needs a different type of setting.

◄ Octagonal cut stones require special prongs that can be closed over the small facets at the stone's corners.

◄ In this piece by Carles Codina, an irregular topaz has been set using the figure of an angel whose arms and chest were carefully fit to serve as a setting.

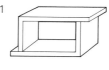

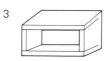

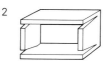

►The sequence involved in making a setting for a rectangular stone, which you can use as is (figure 4), or to which you can solder rectangular wires, as shown in figure 5.

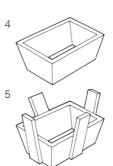

▼ 1. For a bi-colored stone such as this one, prepare a .6 mm sheet, with a shape cut out to fit the culet of the stone. File the interior of the cut out so that the stone fits correctly. Make a 1 mm square wire, and bend it into two right angles, soldered together as shown here. Cut off the excess wire that juts out the sides.

▼ 2. Make a small tube, and solder it along the center of the wire rectangle's longest side. Once soldered, saw off the exterior ends flush, and saw off the ends of the interior tube. In this photo, note how the culet sits in the sheet.

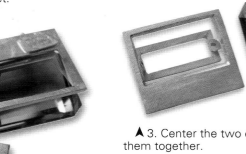

▲ 3. Center the two elements and solder them together.

◄ 4. Make the prongs from a rectangular wire of .8 mm and, after having carefully measured the dimensions of the stone, solder them to the sheet according to the size needed.

▲This is the final result with the stone in its setting.

► 5. Once all the elements have been soldered together, fix the piece in dopping wax, and make a notch in each prong with a bur. Then, press the prongs over the stone with a prong pusher, and shape them with a file. Give the piece its final finish.

Bead Setting

This method of stone setting is very common for both a single stone and the creation of a *pavé setting*—a surface covered with many stones. The technique consists of lifting a small spur of metal from the surface with a special graver, pushing it over the stone, and then shaping it into a bead with a beading tool, leaving the stone completely secured.

▼ Bead setting is very useful for enriching the surface of a piece. Note the details in this piece of jewelry from the collection of Lluís Masriera.

◄ The surface doesn't always have to be flat. Bead setting can be applied to other shapes as well, such as demonstrated in these three rings by Alexandra Siege.

▲ 1. Make a small hole with a drill bit and then, with a ball bur of the same diameter as the stone to be set, enlarge the hole so that the stone fits perfectly into the interior.

▲ 2. With an onglette graver, lift a spur on each side of the stone, as shown in the photo. Lightly push the graver down into the metal so as to press the metal toward the stone and then lift it up so that the metal rests on top of the stone.

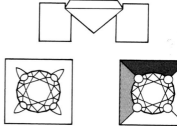

▲ 3. Once the spur is lifted and secured onto the stone, use a flat graver to eliminate the cut marks. This forms a square shape with the stone in the center.

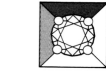

➤ 4. After carving the square shape around the stone with a flat graver, use a beading tool of the appropriate size to lightly round off the spur, using a twisting motion of the wrist.

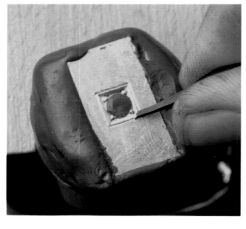

▲ 5. Finally, with a very fine onglette graver, define the exterior of the square.

Pavé Setting

Pavé settings done in gold, especially white gold set with diamonds, is a method that makes a surface look as if it were completely covered with diamonds. The example here is probably the most common, but others exist as well.

➤ 1. Make a series of holes, then enlarge them as needed with a round bur the same size as the stones to be used. This makes the bearing in the same way as shown for bead setting. The stone should fit exactly in the interior (see the illustrations, figures 1 and 2).

➤ 3. In addition to the four spurs situated on top of each stone, make decorative spurs between the stones, using a beading tool to round each of them (see illustration, figure 5)

▲ 2. Once seated, use a fine onglette graver to lift four spurs on each stone in a crisscross pattern using a downward, then upward, movement as shown in the illustrations, figures 3 and 4.

▼ The execution of a pavé setting

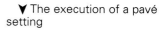

1

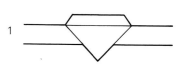

2

3

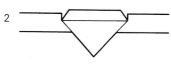

4

➤ This is the final result of the pavé process.

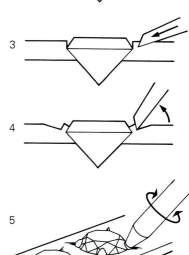

5

WAX MODEL CARVING AND LOST WAX CASTING

As noted in previous chapters, precious metals have common characteristics, such as malleability and oxidation. They can also be melted into a liquid and hardened again into a different state. This knowledge about metal, together with its symbolic content, provided a foundation for working with metals that arose spontaneously in practically every culture. Precious metals were first worked cold, and without being alloyed. Then, thanks to the knowledge acquired primarily through ceramics, we developed better ways to control temperature, and developed the technique of alloying. The invention of the closed kiln (4,000–3,000 B.C.E.), with which even higher temperatures were made possible, was fundamental. Around 3,000 B.C.E., the process of alloying was developed so that we no longer had to work with metal in its pure form, which then gave rise to the development of other, more diverse techniques.

Modeling with Wax

Up to this point, we have shown how to fabricate precious-metal jewelry directly, but there are other means of obtaining pieces and metal objects—for example, with modeling wax, later casting them in metal. Wax modeling can be used to create jewelry and other metal objects with relative ease and speed. No specific knowledge about jewelry making is required to achieve satisfactory results with the technique of lost wax casting. Furthermore, the technique is suitable for producing a small series of pieces at a low cost. If lost wax casting equipment is not available, send wax models to a casting specialist.

▼ Soft waxes are not as hard as carving waxes; they are more like modeling clay. They come in sheet or wire form, in all sizes and shapes. Wax melts easily, making it ideal for joining multiple elements.

▲ Rings designed in modeler's wax, by Jimena Bello

Modeling Waxes

The variety of waxes available for use in this technique all possess certain characteristics that distinguish them from other waxes. They have a higher melting point, around 115°C, and a viscosity superior to that of injection waxes. But they also share a characteristic common to all waxes: once they burn off inside the mold, they don't leave any residue—a deciding factor for good results in lost wax casting.

Each manufacturer makes waxes with certain properties and colors. Finding a wax suitable for your work requires some experience.

◄ A great variety of prefabricated waxes are generally available: sheets, wires, rings of different shapes and sizes, as well as waxes with special characteristics for different types of work.

➤ Apply designer's wax by heating a fine-tipped waxworking tool and applying the hot wax on top of another, more resistant wax. This type of wax is meant for precise work, touchup, and for delicate pieces. Use very fine wax tools with this work.

Basic Tools

A variety of other tools are needed to model with wax. Tools especially made for modeling can be found in a specialized store, but it is much more economical and effective to make tools according to the type of work to be done.

This is especially true with the wax working tools, whose different shapes are important to the work.

There are files especially made for filing wax, or old files no longer used on metal can be utilized, since wax will clog the file and ultimately ruin it for future metal use.

Use different sandpapers for initial sanding, reducing the grade as the piece reaches a smooth finish. Cutting burs of different shapes and sizes—particularly round—will be needed.

For cutting, spiral wax blades that fit in a jeweler's saw are especially useful, as well as a surgical scalpel with a triangular blade. There are also specific buffing products, but for simple work, rub the surface with a cotton cloth and a little lighter fluid, being careful not to round off any edges.

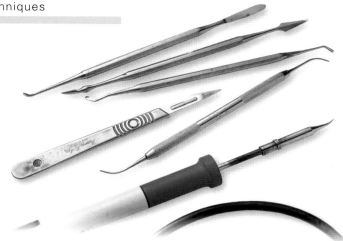

▲ A wax pen is a necessary tool that can be made from a modified soldering iron. Use low heat so that the wax does not boil.

◄ Dental tools can be used to work on bigger pieces, but make some yourself, with finer points for more delicate and precise work, as shown in this photo. These tools have been made from old files, annealing their points and shaping them into the desired form.

Carving Wax

This is a hard wax that comes in compact blocks. Use a spiral sawblade and files to cut out shapes. Because of its special characteristics, hard wax can be bonded together, and allows work with burs and waxworking tools, as well as polishing equipment.

▲ Shape carving wax by any mechanical means—filing, sanding, or using burs. A wax's hardness varies, depending on the manufacturer. There are usually three kinds, and these should be experimented with to determine which works best with what type of work.

◄ Take off the plastic paint and color the line marked into the wax with a correction-fluid pen.

➤ To make a ring from a bar of wax, adjust the interior fit with a ring tube sizer. This tool has a knife edge that makes a concentric cut in the interior of the wax.

▲ To mark the wax, paint the surface with plastic paint and let it dry. Draw or trace a drawing on the paint and then go over the drawing again with a pointed tool, to scratch the lines more deeply into the wax.

Making Rings with a Manual Mini-lathe

A wax lathe is a tool that can facilitate making preparatory shapes, as well as allow for the fast and precise forming of final shapes. There are at least two types of manual mini-lathes on the market. In this section, we will take a very general look at two basic operations that can be performed with a *manual mini-lathe*.

➤ 1. To make a ring on the lathe, first cut the interior to the size needed. Place the knife on the inside of the wax ring tube and turn the lathe in a clockwise direction. The cut will be perfectly straight and precisely measured. This cannot be done on a mandrel since the mandrel's conical shape would be transferred to the interior of the wax.

◄ 2. Placing the piece in the L shaped attachment and resetting the same knife on the exterior of the lathe, cut the outside diameter of the ring.

▼ 3. This equipment is sold with various-sized knife attachments in the shape of a half-moon. The pieces are of brass and can be easily made on your own.

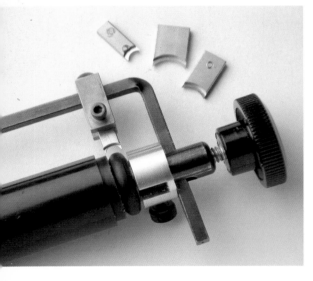

◄ 4. For cutting the ring blank off the wax tube use a graver, or any cutting tool that can be inserted into the support, and turn the lathe while applying pressure.

◄ 5. This is the result obtained by the lathe. From this point, work with other accessories, other types of lathes, or by hand.

➤ Hexagonal rings in wax and in gold

Modeler's Wax

This wax is available in sheets of different thicknesses and with distinct characteristics. Wax in block form is also available; once softened, it can be worked like modeling clay. Ready-made wax wires in different shapes can also be found.

Objects in Modeler's Wax

In the following project, Jimena Bello presents a collection of pieces made from modeling beeswax. At room temperature this wax can be easily manipulated, or heated with a propane canister torch to soften it even more.

▲ You can cut this wax easily with scissors or a craft knife. By holding it over the heat of a propane canister torch, it becomes more malleable, allowing for the creation of more gestural form. This wax can also be soldered, but it is difficult to file.

▲ For sheets that are to be cast later, select a thickness according to the type of piece. We used a thickness of .9 mm. If we had used .5 mm, it probably wouldn't have been a successful casting.

▲ 1. Special modeler's wax can be used, but in this case we are using modeling beeswax that is less expensive and easier to mold. It also leaves no residue when it melts.

▲ 2. Cut a piece of wax and roll it into a wire with the palm of your hand. Flatten the wire and create the shape shown in the photo. Use a craft knife to cut it.

▼ 3. Next, mold the wax object with your hands, and with the help of a waxworking tool, make an opening at the top end.

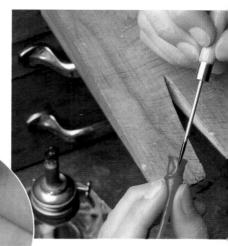

▲ 4. To melt the two pieces together, heat a pointed tool with an alcohol lamp and touch it lightly to the edges of both pieces.

◄◄ 5. With a ball-shaped tool, make an opening at the other end and shape it by hand.

◄ 6. Make four leaves and melt them to the top of the piece, as explained in step 4.

◄ 7. When the wax model is finished, take it to a professional casting specialist who can finish the piece in silver for a reasonable price.

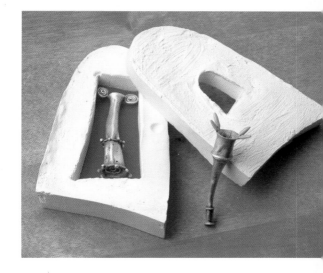

➤ This is one possible result. Piece by Jimena Bello

Hollow Models Using Water-Soluble Wax

This technique uses two kinds of wax. The first is a water-soluble wax, used to form the core of the piece. This core is then covered with the second wax, which will be the model of the desired shape. Once the inner core has been dissolved in water, only the hollow outer wax model will remain.

◄ 1. This kind of wax can be cut, filed, and sanded. Once it's modeled, insert one end of a waxworking tool into the wax in order to handle it in steps 2 and 3.

▲ 3. While submerging the tool with the wax core into the liquid wax, turn it gently so that the wax covers the core evenly.

◄ 4. When cool, remove the tool, leaving a hole in the outer wax. When placed in water, the soluble wax dissolves through this hole.

▲▲ 2. Cover the core with any wax wire, sheet, or other wax form. Here, the core is being coated with liquid wax.

➤ 5. The interior was eliminated, leaving only the outer wax. After casting, a patina was applied to these pieces.

Room Temperature Vulcanizing

There are many materials that cannot be used to make molds for lost wax casting, either because they can't be used with silicone mold release spray, or because they can't be vulcanized. This is true of a tree leaf, a chunk of wall from an old building, or, as we will see, the texture of human skin. We must use a kind of silicone that vulcanizes at room temperature; this allows us to make a direct and immediate negative shape. This silicone is used by dentists to make dental molds.

Making a Brooch

In the same way a dentist would, we use two types of silicone: the green silicone is capable of better definition, while the pinkish-red silicone is both dense and durable. This silicone, carried by dental suppliers, is completely harmless on human skin.

➤ 3. Next, without stopping, mix the second two-part silicone by hand for less definition, until the entire mass is a uniformly rosy color.

➤ 4. Apply this on top of the green silicone to give more volume, weight, and durability to the mold. Press the two together with your fingers.

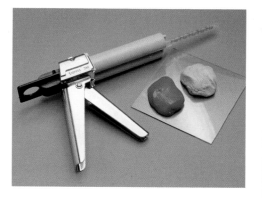

▲ 1. The two-part silicones begin to vulcanize as soon as they are mixed so they should be kept separate until just before the moment of application.

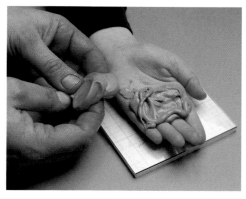

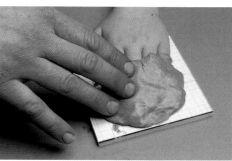

➤ 8. Pour hot wax into the mold. Use either wax from a wax injector, or melt injection wax in a pan, at a temperature of no more than 70°C. Avoid introducing air bubbles that could ruin the model to be cast.

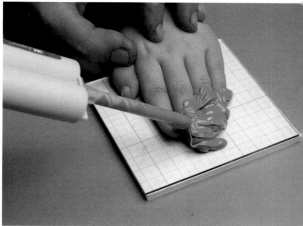

▲ 2. The model used here is a human hand. The first application is made with the silicone that creates high definition, made of two products that vulcanize when mixed. For this reason, we use this applicator that allows both components to mix together uniformly and quickly just at the moment of application. This is done on a smooth surface such as glass.

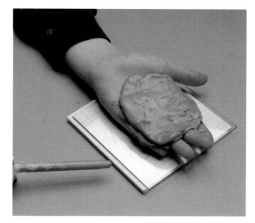

▲ 5. Vulcanizing at room temperature takes approximately five minutes, during which time you should not move your hand.

◄ 6. After five minutes, lift off the mold with care.

▲ 7. The molds can be used over and over again, and there are hundreds of possibilities for getting distinctly different models.

▲9. When the hot wax comes into contact with the cold surface of the mold, it solidifies immediately. To ensure that the surface is evenly covered, pour the wax and move the mold around so that it flows over the whole surface.

▲10. Once the wax has penetrated every corner of the mold, pour off any excess wax that is still hot.

▲11. Once the wax is removed from the mold and while it is still slightly warm, carefully select and cut the pieces you want to work with.

◄ 13. Attach a wax sprue to each piece so that it can be mounted on the main sprue to be cast. To calculate how much the wax will weigh in metal, multiply the weight of the wax by the specific gravity of the metal (15.5 in the case of gold, and 10.5 for silver).

▼ 14. The possibilities are endless using this kind of silicone; here are some of the results from a wax casting.

▲12. The cut pieces are still very thick and irregular on the backside, which will cause an excess of gold or silver to be used in the casting process. Scrape off as much excess wax as you can from the reverse side with a wax working tool, as shown in the photo.

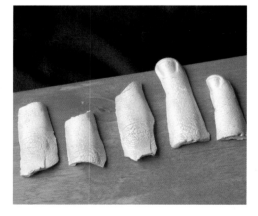

◄ 15. A piece of the palm has been cast in gold. The definition of the skin texture is perfect.

▲ 16. Make a brooch frame with rectangular wire and a sawn-out frame.

▼17. Solder sheet metal as a backing material and rivet the textured casting to the piece, taking care not to ruin the photograph in the interior of the brooch.

➤ Brooch by Carles Codina

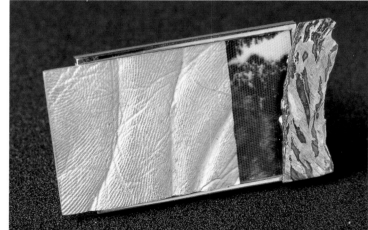

Lost wax casting is a process that begins with a wax model and ends with the finished product in metal. The process encompasses the construction of a metal model, creating the molds, and the subsequent cast reproductions. In the explanation that follows, we have used the simplest and most economical casting equipment available. With similar equipment and a little experience, you can get excellent results. Today there is a lot of inexpensive equipment on the market, but if you don't have the means to purchase it, you can take your models to a casting specialist who can provide you with the final product in whatever metal you specify.

▼ Models with various types of sprue design

The Model for Reproduction

The initial model need not be made of metal. In many cases, as we demonstrated in the previous section, natural elements, such as leaves or twigs, or any other material may be used to make a mold. This opens up so many possibilities that we will limit our demonstration here to the use of a metal model, which is the most commonly used material and one that can be vulcanized. We will also deal with making molds and casting, which make it possible to create many reproductions from the original model. The model could be something made especially for the technique of casting, or it could be an object not originally intended for this purpose. A series of exact reproductions—just a few or many dozens—is made from the model. It is particularly important that the model be carefully prepared because any defect it may have will be faithfully reproduced in the copies.

Characteristics of a Metal Model

The model should be of a uniform thickness. It cannot contain any lacquers, enamels or any other substances that can't be vulcanized. It must also be clean of oxidation and in perfect condition.

One of the most important factors to keep in mind when making a metal model is the reduction of size that will occur in the subsequent wax model. There is no fixed rule for calculating the exact percentage of this reduction. It can be anywhere from 3–11 percent of the original depending on the type of material used for the mold, and especially the dimensions of the piece to be reproduced. Proportionately, a larger piece, such as a brooch, reduces more than a thin ring. Vulcanized rubber also shrinks more than some silicones.

Another important factor to keep in mind is whether the model can be easily extracted after it is vulcanized. Avoid using hollow models or extremely thin ones, especially sheets less than .6 mm.

Sprues

Make sure the sprues are large enough and placed correctly so as to allow the injected wax to enter with ease. If they are too narrow or at the slightest angle the wax will not inject into the mold properly.

Polishing a Metal Model

We don't usually polish the edges or planes of metal models because the polishing process tends to round them. Instead, use a very fine grade polishing stick—normally 1,200. When dealing with complex volumetric shapes, polish the piece and then immerse it in a bath of nickel or rhodium plating before making the mold.

➤ To make molds, use a small machine called a vulcanizer that, using pressure and heat, vulcanizes either a silicone or a rubber material so that it forms a perfect mold around the model.

Creating a Vulcanized Mold

Once the original model is ready, choose materials for creating the mold. There are silicones that vulcanize at room temperature, allowing the use of wood, or any material that cannot be subjected to heat, and a type of transparent silicone exists that allows the model to be seen through the mold.

Here we will be dealing with two of the most common types of vulcanizable molds, silicone and rubber.

Rubber Molds

The material for making rubber molds comes in sheets that should be cut to tightly fit the interior of an aluminum frame. Remove the protective plastic covers from the rubber sheets, leaving the outside covers on the first and last sheets. Pack the frame by first placing half of these sheets face up in the frame, handling them only by the edges. Next, place the model so that the sprue fits into the sprue hole, located at one end of the frame. Continue packing the frame by putting the remaining sheets face down on top of the model. The rubber should fit very tightly, filling the frame just slightly more than it will comfortably hold. Next, sandwich the rubber between two thin sheets of steel so that when heated the rubber will not adhere to the plates of the vulcanizer.

Preheat the vulcanizer to 100°C, insert the frame between the plates, and close the vulcanizer. Raise the temperature to 150°C and close the vulcanizer even more tightly. Tighten it a couple more times during the first five or ten minutes. The increased temperature and pressure forces the rubber to mold around the contours of the model, creating a perfect impression. Allow about seven minutes for every 3 mm of rubber thickness. In this example it would take about one hour to vulcanize. After the allotted time has passed, turn down the vulcanizer and wait until it has cooled to a temperature of 100°C before removing the frame.

4. Always let the rubber come up over the level of the frame just a bit so that the pressure of the vulcanizer will squeeze the mass of rubber very tightly, creating a good impression of the model.

▲1. It is important to cut the rubber for a precise fit so that there is no free space around the piece, because rubber doesn't conform to the model as well as silicone.

➤ 2. Before packing the frame, soften the two rubber sheets that will be in direct contact with the model by preheating them in the vulcanizer for a few minutes at a temperature of 100°C. This will help the material adapt more easily to the contours of the model.

▲ 5. Put the frame between the two sheets of steel and place it inside the vulcanizer that has been preheated to 150°C.

◄ 7. To extract the model from the interior, cut the mold in half, starting at the sprue and continuing to the center. Take great care not to damage the impression of the model.

➤ 8. Cut the outside edges with a zigzag cut to prevent the two halves of the mold from shifting during the injection stage of the process.

◄ 3. Next, take off the plastic protectors. Put half of the rubber sheets inside the frame. Place the model in the middle, as centered as possible, and continue packing the frame with the remaining sheets.

▲ 6. Next, close the press so that the rubber is tightly trapped inside the aluminum frame.

Silicone Molds

Rubber is more economical than silicone, but it doesn't give as clear an impression of the model. Silicone mold rubber is faster and easier to use, both in the preparation of the mold as well as in its extraction. Silicone is also more flexible and adapts to the contours of a metal model much better.

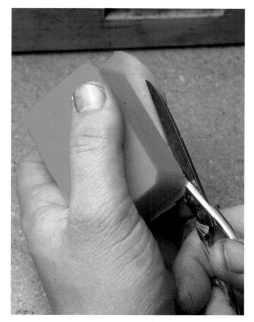

◄ 1. Silicone requires a higher temperature in the vulcanizer, but the process is faster and results in a better impression of the model.

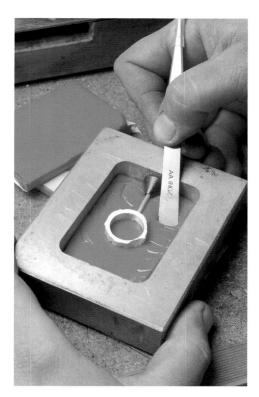

◄ 2. Use a tweezer handle to ensure that the silicone fits tightly into the aluminum frame and around the model.

◄ 3. As with rubber, it is important to make the level of the silicone slightly higher than that of the frame to create pressure around the model in the vulcanizer.

▲ 4. Vulcanize the silicone at 160°C and let it cool. Trim any excess material around the mold.

▼ 7. As you reach the model, make sure to cut on one side or the other of the model's center line so as not to affect the impression when injecting the wax.

▲ 5. Next, remove the sprue, if you have used an extractable one.

▲ 6. It is much easier and faster to cut silicone than to cut rubber.

Injecting the Wax

After cutting open the mold and extracted the model, inject wax into the mold to make wax reproductions identical to the original model. The mold can be reused to make as many reproductions as needed.

Injection wax is a type of wax created specifically for the process of lost wax casting and it melts at 65–75°C. There are many different kinds of injection wax, but in a small workshop where all kinds of pieces can be cast, it is best to use a wax of medium elasticity.

Set the wax injector thermostat to 65–75°C. Make sure the wax doesn't boil, because boiling creates air bubbles that can result in defects in the cast piece.

Air pressure is essential for wax injecting; it enters the wax injector by way of a compressor or a manual pump, and provides the force with which the wax is injected into the mold.

▲ 1. Injection wax usually comes in the shape of small pellets or flakes of various colors. Consult the manufacturer's instructions for specific recommendations.

➤ 2. The injector heats the wax to the thermostat's temperature. The hand pump creates the air pressure that injects the hot wax into the mold.

▼ 3. Pressing the mold up to the injector valve forces wax into the mold.

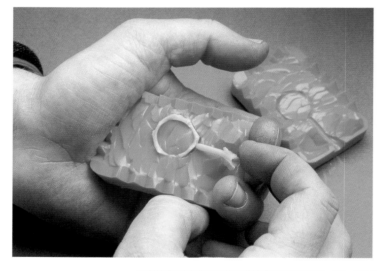

◄ 4. Wait a few moments for the wax to cool, then carefully separate the mold.

➤ 5. The wax copy is always a little smaller than the original model due to contraction of the mold.

Tree Spruing

With tree spruing, multiple wax pieces are connected by their sprues to a main sprue. They are cast in investment material when the wax is melted, leaving an exact copy of the wax model. This process forms the mold into which the melted metal will later be poured. The individual wax models should never touch each other. Begin by attaching the pieces to the top of the main sprue, using the smallest pieces first, and working down the *tree*, making sure all the pieces are attached at an angle no greater than 45°. Put the thicker wax pieces around the bottom of the main sprue, keeping them away from the sprue base.

▲ 1. After finishing all the wax pieces, check them individually and make any necessary corrections. Then mount them to the main sprue starting at the top with the smallest pieces.

➤ 2. Form the main sprue by injecting wax into a piece of rubber tubing, previously cut for easy extraction.

▲ 3. Using a wax pen, cut the main sprue to the desired height, and attach it to the rubber base.

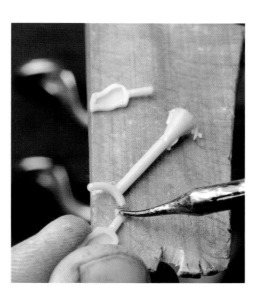

◀ 4. With the same wax pen, shorten the sprues on the pieces to be cast. They shouldn't be very long.

➤ 5. Attach the pieces to the main sprue at a minimum angle of 45°, placing the shorter pieces at the top and the thicker ones at the bottom. Make sure they are secured with the wax pen.

Calculating the Weight of the Metal

Before beginning the investment process, determine how much metal is needed for the casting. To do this, first weigh the sprue base upon which will be attached the main sprue and the pieces to be cast. After attaching the main sprue and all the pieces, weigh it again, and subtract the original weight of the base from the total. This is the weight of the wax. Multiply this number by the specific gravity of the metal to be used in the casting.

The waxes used have a specific gravity very near to 1 so for all practical purposes,

the tree may be weighed and its weight multiplied by the specific gravity of the metal that is to be used in the casting. To allow for the size of the sprue button, add 15 or 20 grams more. For pure silver, multiply the weight of the wax by 10.5. For 18-karat gold, multiply by 15.5. For example, for a base with a wax tree to be cast in gold that weighs 8 grams, multiply the weight by 15.5. To the total of 124 grams, add 15 grams more for a final total of 139 grams of 18-karat gold.

➤ For example, if the weight of the wax is 5.4 grams, multiply this weight by 15.5 when using 18-karat gold. Add 15 grams more for a total of 98.7 grams of gold that you will need to prepare and place in the injector crucible for casting.

Investment and Flask Preparation

Investment is a mixture of plaster and silica, plus chemical modifiers in lesser proportions. The silica is the key element because it facilitates the elimination of gases, controls the expansion, and keeps the investment from contracting.

Careful preparation of the investment is essential. Its purpose is to "invest" or surround the wax tree; once the wax is burned out in the oven, it leaves a hollow space in the mold for the injection of the melted metal. Mix the investment with a ratio of three to four parts distilled or deionized water to ten parts of investment.

◄ 1. Before pouring the investment, paint wetting solution onto the wax tree to reduce the chance of flaws caused by air bubbles when filling the flask.

▼ 2. Insert the steel flask in the rubber base; make a wall around the top of the flask with tape or paper so that the investment doesn't spill during the vacuum process.

▼ 3. The water used to mix the investment should be at room temperature, 20–22°C. The investment sets more quickly if the water is warmer than this and more slowly if it is cooler. In any event, never use water cooler than 15°C.

◄ 4. Next, add the investment. Work quickly, because it will set in eight to ten minutes.

➤ 5. Use an electric beater only at low speed so that air bubbles don't form.

▲ 6. Place the mixture in a vacuum casting machine and vacuum it for the first time to extract any air bubbles.

◄ 7. During this first vacuum, tap the bell jar lightly. The vibration helps eliminate air bubbles.

► 8. Very carefully, and without shaking the mixture, pour the investment into the flask up to the wall of tape. Be very careful not to pour it directly on any of the wax pieces because the weight of the investment may cause them to break off.

▼ 9. Put the flask in the vacuum machine. The level of the investment will rise a few millimeters and splatter slightly. After one minute, continue for another minute more at a pressure of approximately 26, lightly tapping the side of the bell jar. Turn the machine off and allow the pressure to descend slowly by itself until it is completely equalized.

◄ 10. Before the investment sets, make sure that none of the pieces have broken away from the main sprue. If there is one, take it out and subtract its weight from the total weight of the tree. Let the flask sit for two hours before moving it. When the investment has set, take off the tape and scrape off the excess investment with a knife so that it is level with the flask. Twist off the rubber base and place the flask in the oven with the sprue opening facing down.

Calculating the Investment

When casting for the first time, it is important to determine the proportion of water to investment required for a particular size of flask, or refer to charts available from the investment manufacturer. Save the recipe for each flask size for future use.

With the rubber base of the flask attached, fill it halfway with water and then add 20–25% more. It is better to use too much investment than not enough. Measure the depth with a metric ruler and convert to cubic centimeters. Next, multiply by 100 and divide by the proportion of water that the manufacturer recommends (usually 39–42%).

Example: we have water in a flask that measures 300 cc:

$$\frac{300 \times 100}{40} = 750 \text{ grams of investment}$$

750 grams of investment and 300 cc of water are needed.

The proof is obtained by the reverse:

$$\frac{750 \times 40}{100} = 300 \text{ cc of water}$$

Burnout Process

Place the flask in a programmable burnout oven. The heat will eliminate the wax so that metal can later fill the space left by the wax. This type of oven is programmed to automatically increase, maintain, and reduce the temperature necessary for the wax to melt and the investment to heat properly. The heat curve—a sequence of temperature changes—first eliminates all the moisture from the flask, and then melts the wax from the interior. Then, a carbon residue is formed which hardens the investment, making it ready for the final casting process. The elimination of moisture is an especially critical step. The temperature must be regulated very carefully in the first few hours to keep the investment from cracking.

The heat curve will vary, according to the casting metal to be used and the size of the flask. A large flask requires more time to stabilize after each rise in temperature since it takes longer for the heat to reach its interior. The time it takes to reach each stage in the series of temperature changes can take anywhere from 45 minutes for a small flask to one hour for a medium-sized flask, and up to two hours for a large one.

With the equipment described in this chapter we used the following heat curve:

- First hour: raise slowly to 100°C
- Second hour or longer: maintain at 100°C
- Raise another 100°C each hour until reaching 400°C in three hours
- Maintain 400°C for a half hour
- Raise from 400–750°C within 30–60 minutes
- Maintain at 750°C for a time that will depend upon the size of the flask
- Reduce to between 450–600°C depending on the metal to be used
- Maintain at this temperature for a minimum of one hour—longer depending upon the size of the flask

Casting the Metal

To cast melted metal, the temperature of the flask must be lowered to a certain temperature and then kept at that temperature after removing it from the oven. This temperature is determined by the type and fineness of the metal being cast. For gold, maintain the flask's temperature at 500°C for at least one hour before removing it from the oven. Gold may be cast at temperatures ranging from 450–600°C. For silver, cast at 100°C less than the temperature necessary for gold.

Casting metal is one of the most delicate processes in jewelry making. It is best to burn out and cast the materials at the lowest temperatures possible. Avoid overheating the metal, which makes it too porous and ruins the casting.

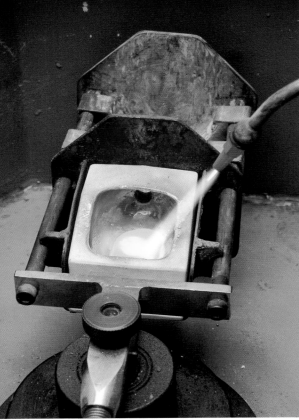

▲ 1. Melt the proper amount of metal in the crucible of a centrifugal casting machine until it is completely liquid.

➤ 2. After the burnout process is complete, take out the flask with tongs and put it carefully in the casting machine.

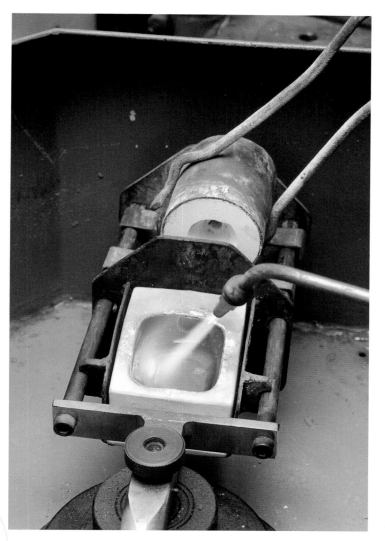

◄ 3. Place the flask in the cradle and reduce the flame of the torch so that the metal stays melted but slightly lower in temperature.

▲ 4. With the counterweights properly balanced and the flask in place, start the machine spinning. Centrifugal force flings the metal into the flask.

➤ 5. Once the metal has been injected, let the flask rest in place for a few moments and then submerge it all at once in cold water. The thermal shock will cause the investment to break apart.

▼ 6. Free the metal from the investment and eliminate the oxides by pickling. The result will be a perfect copy of the original wax tree, now in gold or silver.

➤ 7. Cut the pieces of metal from the main sprue with a sprue cutter. File the sprues off and then sand the pieces with emery paper.

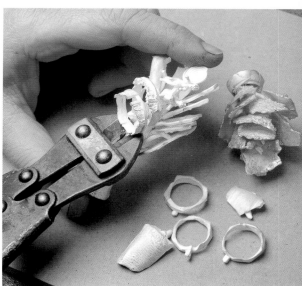

U p to this point, we have been examining the fundamentals of jewelry making and some of the techniques most closely related to it. The craft of jewelry making consists of a great variety of disciplines, each of which has its own body of knowledge requiring its own expertise. In this chapter, we will look more closely at some examples of this expertise in action, and thereby reinforce our earlier instruction in technique. This will allow the reader to see just how multi-faceted the craft of jewelry can be, and at the same time learn the correct methods necessary to plan and fabricate a piece of jewelry. The following projects expand on the techniques and methodology that must be followed in each step, in order to correctly execute each piece. These projects are meant to leave room for the personal and creative contributions of the reader, and it is hoped that they will help all who are interested in the craft of jewelry making.

Step by Step

Repoussé Pendant

Making a pendant constructed of two rounded halves involves the exacting step of tracing a drawing, then making the metal volumetric so that the two halves fit together perfectly to form the body of the pendant.

The chased piece is made from an annealed sheet of silver .7 mm thick. Gold elements are soldered to the lower end of the body and a wire ring is attached to the top so that it can be suspended by a cord or chain. The pendant was made by Carmen Amador.

◄ 3. Heat the surface of the pitch with a low and uniform heat to avoid burning it.

▼ 4. Place the two sheets on the surface of the heated pitch, taking care that air bubbles don't form, and ensuring they are firmly in contact with the pitch.

▲ 1. Select two perfectly symmetrical pieces. To begin, make a drawing on paper that will serve as a template.

▲ 2. Prepare two sheets, .7 mm thick, previously annealed and very clean. Fold down the corners of each sheet with a pair of pliers so that the sheet will adhere better to the pitch.

◄ 5. Let the sheets cool, then attach the drawing with adhesive tape to one of the sheets. With a pointed chasing tool, make small dots along the lines of the drawing until the line is completely delineated with these dots. Do this gently to avoid perforating the sheet. The photo shows the correct way of holding the tool and hammer, which is also very important.

➤ 6. Turn the drawing over to trace it on the other sheet so that when soldering the two pieces together, they will be a perfect match. Note the distinctive shape of the hammer handle in this photo.

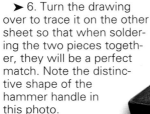

▲ 7. How the hammer and chasing tool are held, as well as your working posture, is crucial in repoussé. Hit the tool with the hammer gently and rhythmically, keeping your hands and elbows up in order to keep the correct angle on the tool. Use your ring finger to guide the tool, keeping it steady under the blows.

◄ 8. Begin to give the piece volume using an embossing punch. Start from the outer edges of the design and work toward the center. Use harder hammer blows so that the metal begins to yield.

▼ 9. Continue the repoussé until the desired volume is reached. Don't worry about the fact that you are working over the dots that you previously marked in the interior. They will not disappear.

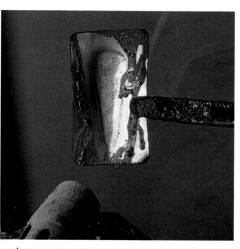

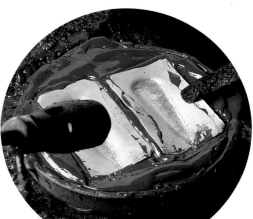

◄▲10 and 11. The metal will become hard to work during the repoussé process. Annealing it will keep it from breaking. Do this as often as is necessary. Apply heat and lift the pieces off the pitch with tongs.

◄ 12. Place the pieces on a soldering block, and anneal the metal until it is soft again.

➤13. During the repoussé process, the outline will eventually need retracing. Put the piece on a bronze block, and use a tracer punch to retrace the line and redefine the shape.

▲14. After redefining the outline, place the pieces back on the pitch and continue the repoussé without losing the shape. Refer to the photo.

▲15. Put the pieces on the pitch again, and continue embossing.

◀ 16 and 17. Keep an eye on the volume by pressing modeling clay into the interior of the piece with a hammer. This technique clearly shows how much volume has been formed.

◀ 18 and 19. Once the desired volume is obtained, remove the pieces from the pitch and anneal and pickle them again. Another way to remove pieces from pitch is to use a chasing tool and hammer as shown.

◀ 20. In order to work the piece now from the opposite or exterior side, it is necessary to put pitch into the interior. Heat the pitch with an alcohol lamp to prevent air bubbles from forming between the metal and the pitch. Air bubbles could cause flaws in the metal.

➤21. Return the pieces to the pitch, with the exterior side up. Use a broad flat tool, called a modeling punch, to smooth and even out the surface.

➤ 22. Turn the pieces over again so that the interior faces up, and go back over the dots with a pointed chasing tool, re-forming their shape.

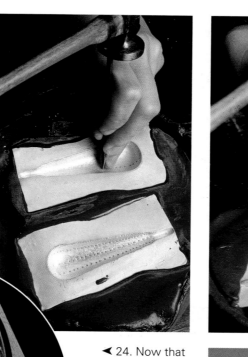

◄ 23. Working from the exterior side again, flatten the dots with a small flat chasing tool to make them more decorative.

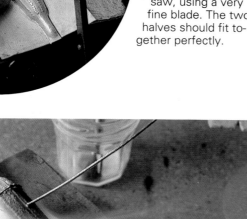

◄ 24. Now that the chasing and repoussé are complete, cut away the excess metal with a jeweler's saw, using a very fine blade. The two halves should fit together perfectly.

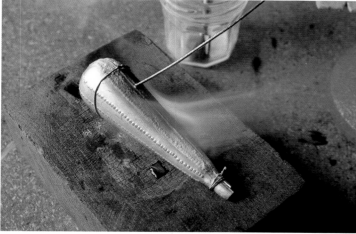

▲ 25. Check the contours, and secure the two halves together with binding wire. Solder the two pieces together, using wire solder and a flame that will completely surround the piece, heating it evenly. Let the solder flow freely over the entire seam. Avoid using too much solder since it will only have to be filed off later. Once the principal solder seam is finished, attach the other gold elements to the pendant.

➤ *Journey III*, by Carmen Amador

Brooch

The following is a brooch that includes techniques introduced in earlier sections of the book. This project will require considerable skill in soldering,, including soldering stone settings and a closure. Setting a good-sized stone, such as the rutilated quartz in this example, will also require some skill in stone setting. The brooch is pure composition—the jewelry format that allows for the most creative freedom. The brooch presented here can be modified to the individual jeweler's taste, but to ensure a good design, always begin by observing the qualities and sizes of the stones you want to use, before making their settings. The rutilated quartz is held in a setting with a gold rectangular wire 1 mm thick by 4 mm wide.

◄ 1. Carefully mark the distances between the corners of the stone on the gold wire. Bevel the marks with a small triangular file so that, when they are bent, the stone will just sit on the metal border, but not inside it.

▲2. Bend the wire at the bevel and solder the ends together. File the exterior and check that the stone can be made to fit in the setting, leaving .3 or .4 mm of metal free above the stone to enclose it.

▲ 3. Although here a round tube is being used, any shape is acceptable. Secure the tube with binding wire, and solder it in place, as shown in the photo.

◄ 4. Prepare a .6 mm sheet with an interior cutout, as shown in the photo. Cut off the excess tubing, and solder the sheet on the tubes, to form a backing for the setting.

▼5. Prepare settings for the other stones.

▼7. A motif of small pieces of bamboo cast in gold is used for this piece.

➤ 6. Here are the two principle settings. The three smaller settings have been joined together with a round wire. This group of three will be connected to the larger setting in the same way.

➤ 8. After determining the composition, fix the elements in place with heat shielding putty so they cannot move during soldering with the water torch. Solder them together, one by one, until the brooch is complete. Remove the oxidation with a pickling acid before soldering the closure.

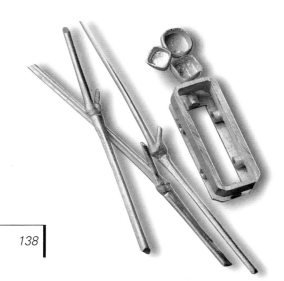

▲ 9. This closure is called a bayonet, and can be purchased from any jewelry supplier. Solder it to the back of the brooch, as shown in the photo.

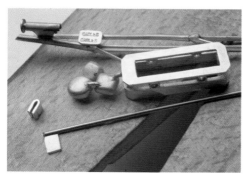

▲ 10. Make the pinstem by soldering a .7 mm unannealed round wire to a .6 mm square sheet. Make a small "U" shape from another sheet that will serve as the support; this is where the pinstem will be attached.

▼ 11. When the round wire is soldered onto the square sheet, it will anneal at the site of the join. To strengthen the wire again, grasp it with a pair of flat pliers, and twist it upon itself. This will restore its temper.

◄ 12. To finish the piece, use an alcohol lamp to heat the dopping wax on a dopping stick, and fix the piece firmly in the wax.

▲ 13. The entire piece should be firmly set in the wax to withstand the pressure and pounding as the stones are set.

▲ 14. With a ball bur, grind the interior shape of the setting, until the girdle of the stone fits securely inside. With a half-round graver, finish the seat, making sure there will be enough excess metal over the stone to enclose it.

▲ 15. Since the culet of the stone is of a better quality than its table, we have set it upside down. Use a bezel pusher to press the excess metal down over the stone to secure it in place.

▲ 16. Go over the edge of the bezel of the setting with a hammer handpiece to tighten and harden the metal.

◄ 17. File the edge to eliminate any excess metal, and then sand it. With a small flat bur supported by the stone, grind out any irregularities that may still exist between the stone and the metal, leaving the edge of the setting completely ready for polishing.

▼ 18. This is the final result after setting the remaining stones, and giving the bamboo motifs a satin finish. *Needle*, by Carles Codina

Articulated Bracelet with Clasp

T he following project consists of the construction of a bracelet with uncut diamonds. The body of the bracelet has been made from a piece of tree bark, cast in gold. It is an extensive project in that it incorporates many of the basic processes of jewelry making: preparing the bark for casting, finishing the cast elements, linking the pieces of the bracelet together, making a box clasp adapted to the design, and finally setting the stone.

▲ 1. Start by breaking the tree bark into pieces and selecting them for their size and texture quality. The best results will come from more markedly textured pieces.

➤ 2. Clean each piece carefully, and file them on the interior side, to make them as thin as possible without breaking them.

▼ 3. It may not be possible to file the pieces completely smooth, or it may be that they are too thin in some places. To rectify this, apply designer's wax with a spatula to both strengthen and smooth out the surfaces.

◄ 4. Mount wax sprues on the pieces, then mount them on a main sprue, and prepare them for casting, as described in the section on lost wax casting (page 116). If casting equipment is not available, take the pieces to a casting specialist.

▲5. When the pieces are cast, cut off the sprues with a jeweler's saw. Since the sprue is fairly thick, use a relatively coarse sawblade, such as a 1 or 2.

▲6. File the interior side of the pieces until the surfaces are very smooth and even.

➤ 7. Sand each piece with successively finer grades of emery paper up to 1,000 –1,200-grit so that the interior is completely smooth.

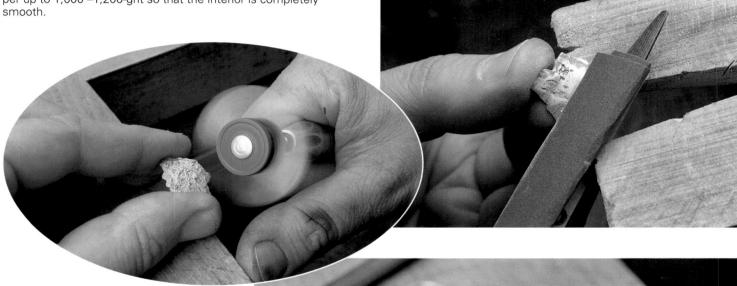

▲ 8. Give the exterior a matte finish, using a satin wire brush attachment on a micro motor, as shown in the photo. This attachment will give the piece a rough-hewn look.

➤ 9. Make the settings for the small, uncut diamond cubes. These are constructed using a .5 mm rectangular wire soldered to a .5 mm sheet, using hard solder. Cut away the excess sheet, and file it smooth and flush to the contour of the wire.

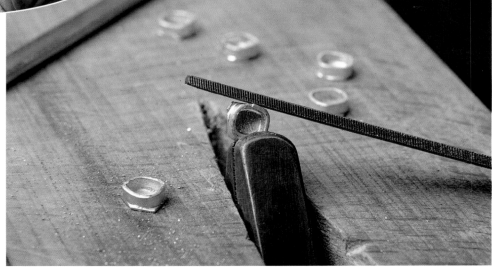

Multi-Section Linkage

To show how this kind of link functions, its construction is demonstrated here, using two rectangular sheets of silver. The movement that this linkage allows functions exactly the same when implemented on the cast pieces.

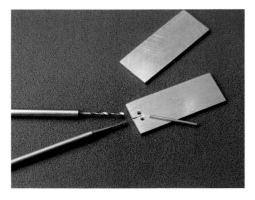

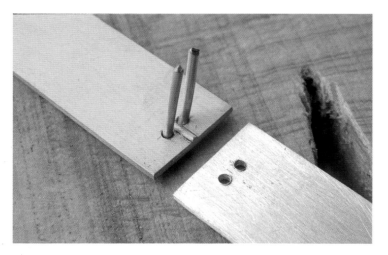

▲1. With a .6 mm drill bit, make two holes at one end of each sheet so that they are no more than 1 mm apart. Then, with a rectangular bur (as shown in the photo), grind out a transversal channel between the two holes on one of the sheets. Solder a .6 mm wire into this channel.

▲ 2. Turn this piece over, and with a slightly larger rectangular bur, grind out the metal between the two holes until the wire on the other side is reached. Bend a wire into a U shape that can be placed into these holes and sit comfortably on the soldered wire.

◄ 4. Insert the U-shaped wire into the holes of both sheets and solder them to the upper sheet.

▼ 6. When the U-shaped wire is soldered, a space is left between the sheets that creates the movement. This small space of separation, together with the hole made by the bur, where the base of the U sits, allows the pieces to move.

▲ 3. The space ground out below the wire, on the underside of the lower sheet allows the linkage to move after it has been soldered—without this space the link would be frozen. In the next step, solder the U to the upper sheet, and link the two sheets together.

▼5. Cut off the excess wire, then file and sand smooth so that there is no evidence of the solder joint.

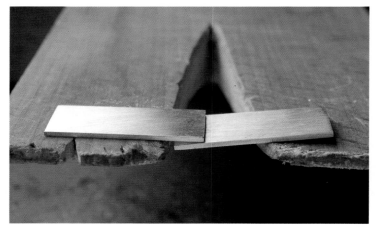

◄ 8. Do not solder the pieces together until the settings have been soldered onto the pieces. Arrange the settings with an eye for composition, but their placement should appear somewhat random. Make sure that the settings don't obstruct the holes.

▲7. Link each piece of the bracelet, using this technique. Make two holes at one end of each piece, solder in a transversal wire, and grind out the metal underneath it. On the other end of each piece make two more holes so that a .7 mm U-wire can be inserted, to link them all together. Link them temporarily, while deciding on their order and composition, to a total length of about 18 cm.

➤ 9. When all the settings have been soldered and the composition is final, link the pieces together again with the U-wires, and pull them slightly so that they are secure.

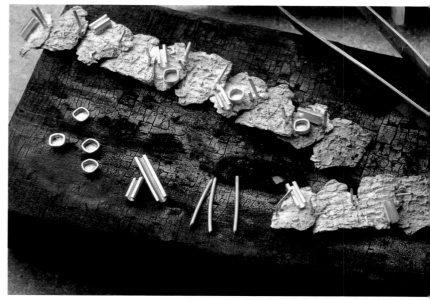

◄ 10. Put the bracelet on a soldering block and, using paste solder and a water torch, solder only one side of the U. Leave the other side free until the movement of the piece is established, as shown as in the next step.

➤11. Hold the bracelet at one end and let the other end hang free. Move the bracelet up and down, to create the movement and ensure that the bracelet will conform comfortably to the wrist. Only after you are assured that it has a fluid movement should you solder the other side of the U-wire.

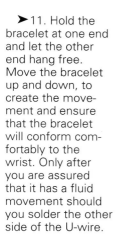

Constructing a Box Clasp

All linked bracelets need a clasp in order to be worn. The box clasp is one of the most common, especially in wide pieces such as the one shown here. It an easy clasp to open and close. It is also secure, easy to construct, and can be adapted to any design.

➤ 1. Prepare several sheets .5 mm thick. From one of these, cut and file a piece that is 5–6 mm wide by 3–4 cm long. At a point 1 cm from one end, make a V-shaped bevel, so that the piece can bend back on itself, thereby forming a tongue.

▲ 2. Before bending the tongue, anneal the sheet so that it doesn't break. Solder the bend with hard solder, then polish with emery paper. Cut a bridge in another sheet that exactly fits the tongue section, as shown in the photo.

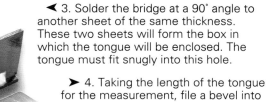

◄ 3. Solder the bridge at a 90° angle to another sheet of the same thickness. These two sheets will form the box in which the tongue will be enclosed. The tongue must fit snugly into this hole.

➤ 4. Taking the length of the tongue for the measurement, file a bevel into the box, then bend up the end of the box at a 90° angle, and solder with hard solder. The box should fit the cast gold piece and form a housing, such as shown in the photo.

▲ 5. Solder the box to the previously cast gold piece at the contact points, using medium solder. File the front of the box so that the box and the piece are flush and smooth.

◄ 6. Solder a piece of sheet or wire at least 1 mm thick to the top of the tongue. Use a jeweler's saw to cut out a fitting for this piece from the box so that the release button and tongue will fit into the interior of the box.

▼ 8. Turn the closure over and solder a piece of the cast gold to the release button on top of the tongue to conceal it.

➤ 7. Make a small U-shaped bridge, beveling and soldering with strong solder so that it serves to support the other end of the tongue. Make this piece the same height as the box so that it will help guide the tongue inside. Solder the tongue to the bridge.

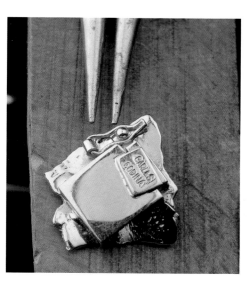

◄ 9. To make a safety clasp mechanism, solder a small ball of gold into a rounded depression on one side of the box. On the other side, solder a small tube, and insert a piece of thin wire. Bend the wire as shown, and solder the ends together.

➤10. With a pair of chain nose pliers, tighten the wires in the center so that the clasp will stay tightly fastened around the ball.

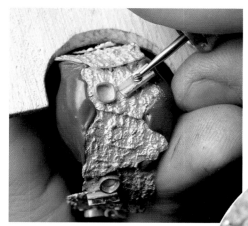

◄12. Uncut diamonds are of irregular sizes so each stone must be fitted separately. With a ball bur, grind out the interior of the channel settings from end to end. With a smaller ball bur, make the seat for the diamonds to fit into.

▲11. Before setting the stones, use a satin wire brush once again, to renew the matte finish on the surface.

➤13. Using a stone setter's tool, place each stone in the channel, leaving enough excess metal above the stones to close the channel over them.

▲ 14. It is possible to close the setting directly with a hammer handpiece, but here the stones are set with a prong pusher. Then the setting will be reinforced with a hammer handpiece.

▲15. Go over the edge of each setting with a graver to smooth out the hammer marks. Once the setting's edges are polished, the piece is finished. Work by Carles Codina

Gold Pendant with Chain

This pendant is permanently attached to its chain. In this section is demonstrated how to make a simple chain from square wire, how to bend a wire to form a right angle, how to solder several elements together, and finally, how to prepare stone settings that complete the body of the pendant. To make the chain, start with a 2 x 2 mm square wire. Construct round jump rings with a 1.3 mm wire (see the chapter Basic Techniques, page 26). For the body of the pendant, make a rectangle using the same square wire, and select textured pieces from tree bark cast in gold. Finally, construct two different types of settings for two different shapes of uncut diamonds.

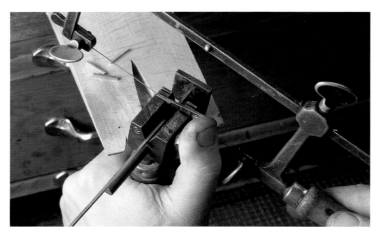

▲ 1. Cut the square wire into a number of 2 cm lengths. Here a tubing cutter jig, fixed to a certain distance, aids in the rapid and accurate cutting of small pieces.

▲ 2. Make about 40 round jump rings with an interior diameter of 1.5 mm, and another 20 with an interior diameter of about 3 mm. The larger rings are used to connect the smaller ones.

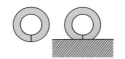

▲ Close the small rings with a pair of flat-nosed pliers and file them flat at the closure. Placing this flat side on the squared wire, solder a ring to either end of each wire as shown in the drawing.

➤ 3. Solder one of the smaller rings to each end of the squared wire pieces. Make sure the rings are aligned, as shown in the photo.

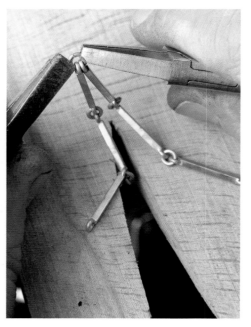

◄ 4. After soldering all the smaller rings, use the larger ones to connect the pieces. Use a pair of flat-nosed pliers to open the rings wide enough to insert the two smaller rings, then close the ring.

➤ 5. The best way to solder the chain links is to lay them on a soldering block, heat up each ring a little bit, apply paste solder to each one, and then immediately solder one after the other.

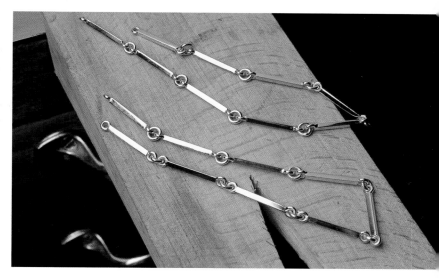

▲ 6. After soldering, pickle the chain, sand it with a fine (1,000–2,000) grade of emery paper, and buff the links using flat buffing wheels and a small silicone polishing point.
To make the body of the pendant, cut two lengths 10 cm each, from the same 2 mm square wire used for the chain.

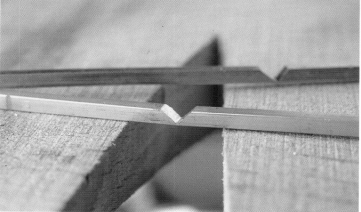

◄ 7. Make a 90° angle in the wires by filing a "V" almost all the way through the wire, as shown in the photo. Anneal the wire so that it is flexible enough to be bent. Bend it into an L shape.

◄ 8. Reinforce the corners with paillons of solder, applying flux first.

▲ The short sides of the L should have exactly the same measurement.

➤ 9. Before soldering the two pieces together to form the rectangle, measure them carefully, making certain they are exactly the same size. Here a vernier caliper is used to measure the short sides. Solder only one side first, then measure again so that if there has been any movement it can still be corrected before soldering the other side.

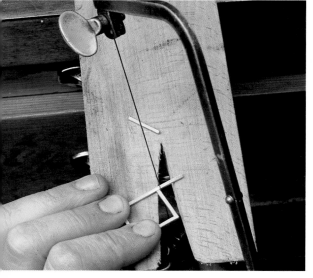

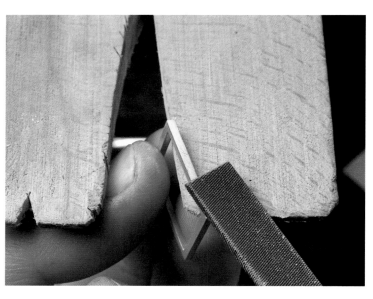

◄ 10. After soldering, saw off the two excess ends of the wire from the rectangle.

►11. File the piece, then sand it with progressively finer grades of emery polishing sticks. Make sure to keep the edges and corners sharp and well defined.

◄ 12. Irregular pieces of tree bark cast in gold were chosen, but another motif would work as well.

►13. Now the elements can be joined to the rectangle of wire. If hard solder was used in the corners of the rectangle, and a water torch is not available, then a medium solder can be used to do this step.

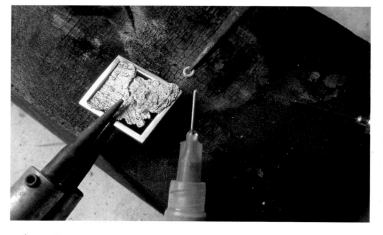

▲ 14. To connect the body of the pendant to the chain, solder two small rings to the upper edges of the rectangle.

► 15. Two types of uncut diamonds are used here; each requires a different setting. The first is simply a channel setting made by bending a small metal sheet on a forming block.

16. The second setting is for a roughly cube-shaped uncut diamond. To set it correctly, a very fine rectangular wire is bent with pliers to form a bezel that conforms to the diamond's particular shape. Once adjusted to fit, solder the ends, then solder a .5 mm sheet to one side, cutting and filing away the excess metal, following the contours of the setting.

◀ 17. The necklace has a clasp at the back. Attach two relatively large jump rings to each end, and on one place a lobster clasp, which can be purchased from a jewelry supplier. Keep in mind that the clasp contains a steel spring that must not be heated, or it will lose its temper and cease to function. Close the jump ring to secure the clasp, but instead of soldering it, use a relatively thick ring that has been only slightly annealed to maintain its strength.

◀ 18. The other diamonds are set in a seat made in the middle of the channel. Because they are uncut, they must be set according to their individual characteristics.

▼ 19. This is the result. All of the rectangular wire was polished to a mirror finish, but the cast elements were given a matte finish with an acid bath.

Multiple Loop-in-Loop Chain

T his chain is constructed of soldered jump rings made from .9 mm silver wire. A thinner or thicker wire might be used, but the best results come from a fine quality of thin wire. The effect can be changed by alternating the silver with rings of other metals. The first step consists of making rings by wrapping wire in a spiral on a jump ring mandrel with a diameter no smaller than 1.5 cm. Cut the rings and solder them, one by one.

▲ 1. Placing the rings on a soldering block in the manner shown in the photo is a very practical and efficient method of soldering the rings quickly. Paste solder is the most appropriate solder form when using a water torch. If using a conventional soldering torch, it is better to use wire solder.

▲ 2. Solder a large quantity of these rings using paste solder and the water torch.

➤ 3. To create the form needed to construct this chain, shape each ring into an oval, using a pair of bent, round-nose pliers.

➤ 4. First, make a base on which to begin working. Construct the base by soldering a piece of heavy, round wire to the middle of two rings, as shown in the photo. A loop-in-loop chain can be made with bases of four, six, or more initial loops.

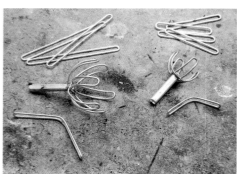

◄ 5. Once the base is made, bend the rings up to form loops. The more rings used in the initial base, the larger the rings must be.

▼ 6. Secure the base firmly in a table vise. Insert a ring in the first set of loops, and with the thumb and forefinger, bend the ring upward into a vertical position.

▼ 7. Use a large rug needle or wire rod to ensure that the loop ends are even on either side as they are bent.

▼ 8. Insert the next ring and repeat the process, moving in a clockwise direction.

◄ 9. It is at this point that the work of threading the loops of the necklace begins, but with one important difference. Instead of inserting the next ring through the highest loop, insert it in the one just below it, taking in two loops, not just one. Bend the ring upward as before, and continue with the insertion of the next ring.

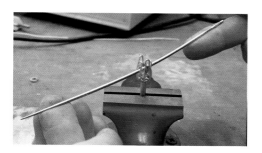

▲ 10. Before inserting each new ring, use the needle to help even out and open up the next pair of loops that will be used to insert the next ring.

▲ 11. Keep repeating the process. First, insert the needle into the second highest pair of loops to open them up, and then insert the ring, bending it upward.

◄ 13. Once finished, stretch the chain through a wire drawplate or a hole drilled in wood. Insert one end of the chain in the hole, and draw it through very carefully with the help of draw tongs. This will even up the loops in the chain, but it will become a bit stiff.

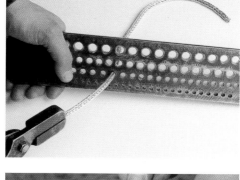

▲ 12. As the necklace grows longer, hold it as shown in the photo. This chain should be made to a minimum length of 40 cm. This kind of corded chain is especially good for making short necklaces, such as chokers. Always allow an additional 2 cm for the clasp.

➤ 14. Use a bracelet mandrel or a wooden rod 5–6 cm in diameter to create flexibility in the chain. Take one end of the chain in each hand, and slide the chain back and forth over the rod, as shown in the photo.

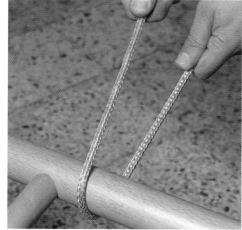

◄ 15. The easiest way to finish the ends is to make chain caps, such as those explained on page 51, and solder them to the chain. Then attach any of the various clasps that can be purchased from a jewelry supplier.

▲ Thicker wires and smaller rings will create a chain that is more compact. This loop-in-loop chain is made of gold.

▼ The same kind of chain can be made using two, three, or more rings. When making a chain with three rings using a wire of the same diameter, the rings themselves should be bigger.

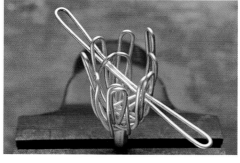

◄ The process is the same as that using two rings…

➤ …but the result is not exactly the same. The shape of the necklace is slightly different.

Hollow-Construction Ring

The following project shows how to make a ring out of silver and gold, set with an unusual stone. It provides a good review of techniques illustrated in previous chapters, since it highlights many important technical aspects, such as beveling, fitting, oxidizing silver, making a screw, and especially soldering. First prepare the body of the ring by beveling, then bending, silver rectangular wires. Next, solder metal sheets to the wire, using the appropriate hardnesses of solder; then file and sand the exterior. Finally, pickle the piece, and make a screw fastener to connect the stone to the piece.

▲1. After pouring a silver ingot, annealing and pickling it, roll it through the rolling mill until it is 1 mm thick. Cut it into two equal lengths; anneal and then pickle, filing them smooth, as described in previous sections.

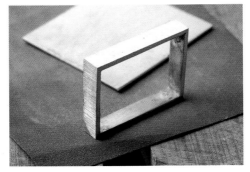

▲2. The framework of the ring is made by beveling the rectangular wires and soldering them together with hard solder. File the exterior so that both sides are smooth and even. Prepare one sheet of gold and one of silver, both .6 mm thick.

▲ 3. With binding wire for soldering, fasten the rectangle to one of the sheets. Make the wire just tight enough so the rectangle won't slide around. If you make the wire tight, it could cause the piece to deform. Apply a little solder inhibitor to the corners to protect the previous seams, but be careful that it does not flow onto places where you will be soldering later.

▲4. Put the piece on a soldering nest so that the flame will pass under as well as over the piece, thus heating it uniformly, allowing the solder to flow easily between the sheet and the rectangle. Since a hard solder was used on the corners, use a medium solder here.

▲5. Saw out a hole in the silver, as shown in the photo, and prepare a .6 mm sheet of gold. Then make a gold ring with the same diameter and thickness as that of the hole just sawn in the silver sheet.

➤ 6. Repeat the soldering operation, using a gold sheet for the opposite side. Protect the previous solder seams, and secure it with binding wire as before.

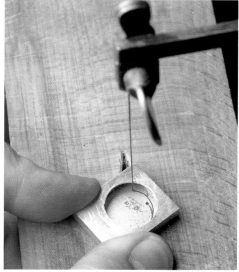

▲ 7. When soldering with paillons, better results are achieved by heating the whole piece a little first, then placing a little soldering flux on the paillons before applying them to the piece. Use medium solder.

▲ 8. Using wire solder, apply flux, and heat the entire piece with a conventional gas torch until it reaches the right temperature; then apply the wire solder.

▲ 9. Eliminate the oxidation with acid, and file and sand the exterior. Next, saw out a hole in the gold sheet exactly the same size as the one sawn out of the silver sheet.

▲ 10. File the interior of the hole with a half-round file, until the gold ring fits perfectly into the space.

▲ 11. After protecting the previous solder seams, place paillons of soft solder around the ring, and apply a uniform flame to the piece.

➤12. Once the last solder join is finished, file off all the excess, and sand, using two or three successively finer grades of emery paper. Be sure to leave all the corners and edges sharp and clear.

◄14. Submerge the ring in silver oxidizer. This will cause the silver to darken without changing the color of the gold.

▲13. At one end of the top of the ring drill a hole and use a tap to thread it. Make the male counterpart that fits into the ring in silver; it also needs to fit into a hole made in the stone.

◄ 15. Finally, attach the stone to the ring.

➤ *Ring with Precious Stone* by Carles Codina

Crocheted Chain

Work done with fine wire can be enormously creative. In fact, by using a good quality wire that is thin enough, the possibilities are endless. The chain presented here is only one of the many different techniques taken from fiber crafts, and is usually done with thread. The technique is easy because it requires only a crochet hook and a fine wire of either gold or silver. With the proper quality and size of wire the technique can be varied, making it possible to create in metal almost anything normally done with fiber.

This work has been created by Tanja Fontane using a .25 mm silver wire. A gold wire of this same size would work equally well.

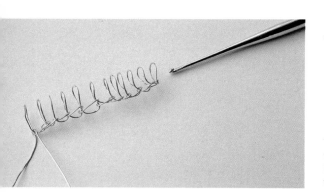

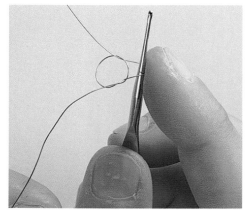

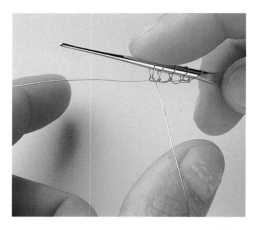

▲1. Start with a spool of annealed silver wire and a small crochet hook. The bigger the hook, the bigger the loop of the stitch, creating a looser chain.

▲2. Begin the work using copper. The first step is to form the initial loops (see step 5); the number of loops at this stage determines the diameter of the chain.

▲ 3. Twelve loops should be formed, as shown in the photo.

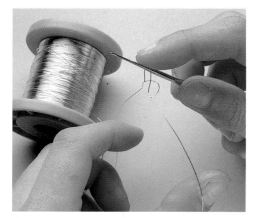

◄ 4. Be very careful to make all the loops evenly spaced and of the same size.

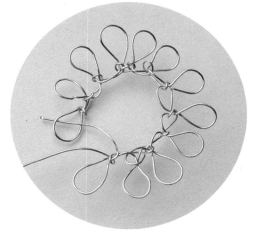

➤ 5. This photo shows the initial stitches. The loops have been turned to lie flat, and then closed, to form a kind of ring that is held on the end of a finger, which ensures that the loops stay the same size.

◄ 6. The long end of the wire connected to the spool must pass through the middle of the first loop from the back side. To do this, insert the hook into the loop, catch the wire from the back, and draw it out, leaving the loop placed over the one it just passed through.

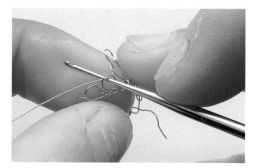

➤ 7. Repeat this process over every loop for several turns.

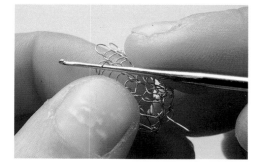

▲ 8. At this point, begin to insert the hook in the second highest loop, rather than the highest one as before. This will create more density and uniformity in the chain and give it a more definite shape.

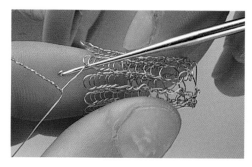

▲ 9. Up to this point, the work has been in copper so that the chain can later be stretched from the ends without breaking. Now exchange the copper wire for silver wire by twisting the two together, as shown in the photo, and continue working as before.

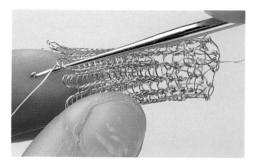

▲ 10. Observe in this photo how the hook is inserted from the outside into the second loop, catching the wire that is running along the inside and pulling it through to the outside, lifting and depositing the loop directly above the loop just worked.

▲ 11. Continue until the chain reaches a minimum length of 40 cm, making sure that the stitches are straight, and that the diameter is as uniform as possible.

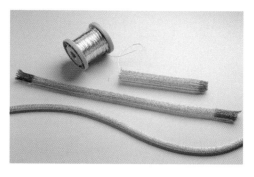

▲ 12. After reaching the desired length, change from the silver wire back to copper (refer to step 9). Choose any type and combination of wires that may be appropriate to the individual design.

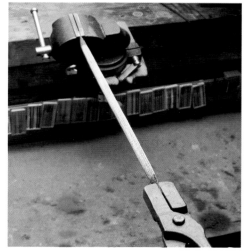

▲ 13. Now grasp both ends of the chain firmly, as shown in the photo, in order to stretch it, strengthen it, and increase its elasticity so that it moves well and drapes nicely on the body.

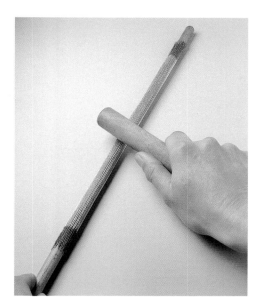

▲ 14. Next, insert a wooden rod inside the chain and, placing it on a flat surface, "brush" the chain over its exterior with long movements, using any circular wooden piece, such as a tool handle.

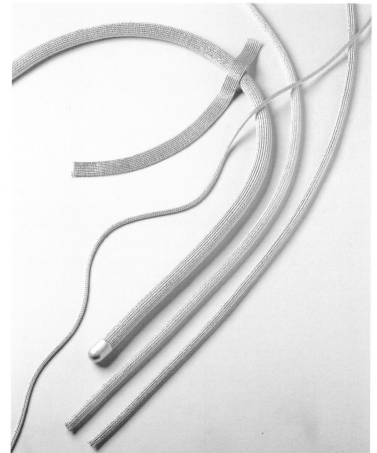

◄ 15. Finish the chain with chain caps, and solder to them any type of clasp you like.

Glossary

a

Alloy. Result of melting two or more metals together.

Annealing. The action of heating metal until it reaches a cherry red color and then letting it cool. Annealing restores malleability to the metal after it has been subjected to a mechanical process, such as rolling or forging.

Aqua regia. Solution of nitric acid and chloride that can dissolve gold.

Arkansas stone. Abrasive stone used to file gravers.

b

Beading tool. Tool in the form of a steel rod with a concave point, used to round off small beads in stone settings.

Bezel pusher. Tool used to close a stone setting over a stone.

Borax. A type of flux; helps solder to flow, and protects metal from oxidizing when heated.

Brilliant cut. Common shape of a cut diamond.

Burnishing. Creating shine on a metal surface by using a special tool, usually made of steel, hematite, or agate.

c

Caliper. Instrument of precision used to calibrate sheets and wires.

Carat. Unit of weight measurement of gemstones, equivalent to .2 grams.

Chasing tool or **punch**. Steel tool that, when tempered correctly, is used to chase metal.

Contaminated gold. Effect produced in gold when it is contaminated by ferrous metals, causing it to crack and become hard.

Counterenamel. Enamel applied on the reverse side of a sheet to counteract the tension created by the enamel applied to the front side.

Culet. Pointed end of a cut stone located on the very bottom of the stone.

Cupel. Porous crucible used in chemical tests to determine the purity of gold.

Cupellation. Method of testing for the purity or standard of a gold alloy.

d

Dopping wax. Paste used to secure a piece in place during stone setting.

Dopping stick. A support, generally made of wood, upon which dopping wax is placed. Used to secure settings when placing or setting a stone.

Drawing bench. A long bench that, together with a drawplate, is used to reduce the diameter of a metal wire.

e

Earring post. In pierced earrings, the small piece of cylindrical metal that passes through the earlobe.

Embossing. Shaping metal by force, using a hammer and chasing tools that usually have rounded ends.

Enamel. Vitreous material made of silica and other elements that adhere to metal at high temperatures.

Enamel flux. A vitreous, transparent material used as an enamel base.

f

Findings. Small, prefabricated pieces used in jewelry, such as clasps and settings.

Flex shaft motor. Motor with a flexible arm attached, through which the action of the motor is transferred to the handpiece.

g

Gemstone cutter. A professional whose expertise is the cutting and faceting of precious stones.

Girdle. Border of a cut stone that separates the pavilion from the crown.

Graver. Steel instrument ending in a point, used by engravers to cut or scratch metals.

h

Horn anvil on base. Type of table anvil used in jewelry that has two lateral pointed ends, one of which is flat.

j

Jeweler's saw. A steel arc, in which a saw blade is mounted and used for cutting.

k

Karat. Unit of measurement, used to express the quantity of pure gold in an alloy.

l

Loss. Losses of metals produced during sawing, sanding, and the like. Much of this loss is recoverable.

m

Maker's mark and **hallmark.** Marks stamped in metal that identify the maker and standard of metal.

Mandrel. Conical steel bar with various sections, used to shape and size rings.

Metal snips. Type of scissors for cutting metal, the smallest of which are used to cut solder snippets, or paillons.

Mica. A mineral that, used in fine sheets, can facilitate the process of granulation.

n

Nitric acid solution. Combination of distilled water and nitric acid, used in various proportions to clean gold, eliminating alloyed metals.

p

Paillons. Small pieces cut from a sheet of solder.

Pickling. Eliminating the oxide on a metal with an acid bath.

Pickling solution. Stripping solution, used to eliminate oxide produced on the surface of metal after annealing or soldering.

Pitch. Substance that allows pieces to be held in place during chasing and repoussé.

q

Quartering. The process of purifying contaminated gold by quartering it with copper and submerging it in nitric acid.

r

Reamer. Tapered steel rod with cutting edges, used to widen holes and clean tubes.

Rosin. Solid, translucent material derived from distilled turpentine; also called Greek pitch. Used to make pitch or lacquer, which holds a piece securely while working it.

s

Saw blade. Mounted in the arc of a jeweler's saw, used to saw or make cutouts in metal.

Solder. Alloy used to join two metals together.

Soldering flux. Liquid that inhibits the formation of oxide and facilitates the soldering process.

Soldering nest. Soldering base, made of iron wire, that allows a uniform flame to surround the piece; also called a jeweler's wig.

Soldering tweezers. Small, heat-resistant tongs, used to hold elements while soldering them. Some have different pressures and shapes.

Sprue hole. The hole located below the main sprue, through which melted wax flows during lost wax casting.

Steel bench block. Flat, machined steel block, used as a work surface at the jeweler's bench.

Stone setter's tool. Tool made of wax and drawing charcoal used to pick up, hold, and place stones in stone setting.

Stone setting. Technique involving fabrication of stone settings and fitting stones within them.

Sweeps. Trash, swept up from the floor in a workshop, that contains metal scraps, which can be recovered.

t

Temper. The point of hardness created in metal by heat or mechanical means.

Touchstone. Hard, black stone used to test gold and silver.

y

Yellow ocher. Solder inhibitor used to protect previously soldered joins from heat.

Index

Bibliography & Acknowledgments

Benavente, Jorge Alsina. *Metals in Modern Jewelry*. Barcelona: Editorial Alsina, 1986.

Kallenberg, Lawrence. *Modeling in Wax for Jewelry and Sculpture*. Radnor PA: Chilton Book Company, 1981.

McCreight, Tim. *Boxes & Lockets*. London: A&C Black, 1999.

McCreight, Tim. *The Complete Metalsmith: an Illustrated Handbook*. Worcester MA: Davis Publications, 1982.

McCreight, Tim. *Jewelry: Fundamentals of Metalsmithing*. Madison WI: Hand Books Press; London: A&C Black, 1997.

McGrath, Jinks. *Encyclopedia of Jewelry-Making Techniques*. Philadelphia PA: Running Press Book Publishers, 1995.

Olver, Elizabeth. *The Jeweller's Directory of Shape & Form*. London: A&C Black, 2000.

Untracht, Oppi. *Jewelry: Concepts and Technology*. Garden City NY: Doubleday, 1982.

I want to extend my appreciation to la Escuela Massana of Barcelona and to all the professors and students who collaborated with me in the production of this book—especially to those who helped me acquire the indispensable professional experience necessary to write this book.

Many people participated in the creation of this work. I want to especially note the contributions of Ramón Puig Cuyàs and Xavier Doménech, who wrote the chapters Contemporary Jewelry, and The Origins of Ornamentation, respectively. Their chapters advance the relevance of contemporary jewelry, giving greater meaning to the book.

Special thanks needs to go to Estela Guitart, for the chapter Urushi (Japanese Lacquer); to Carmen Amador, for the chapter Chasing and Repoussé, and to Joan Aviñó, for her valuable contribution to the chapter Stone Setting. I feel indebted to Verónica Andrade, whose collaboration helped me create the exercises in granulation, and to write various chapters.

I also want to express my appreciation to many professionals and friends for their valuable advice and contributions. Special thanks goes to Joaquim Benaque, for his help with questions pertaining to chemistry; to Jimena Bello, for information on modeler's wax; Tanja Fontane, for creating the chain of rings; Ramón Puig, for help with patinas; Jaime Diaz, for his contributions on forging; and Carme Brunet, for her explanations and commentary on enameling.

I wish to thank all those who offered their enthusiastic and voluntary assistance in this book, especially Aureli Bisbe, towards whom I feel extraordinarily grateful for his help with many chapters, as well as those who contributed their jewelry pieces to the book, which have so enriched its contents.

Thanks also goes to: the Magari Gallery and the Forum Ferlandina Gallery, both of Barcelona, and their directors, Pilar Garrigosa and Beatriz Würsch; the supply company Chamorro and Moreno, and especially Jordi Solsona, an esteemed professional; to Joan Oliveres of the Bagues Firm; Joaquim Capdevila; Judith McCaig; Harold O'Connor; Sybilla; Kepa Carmona; Francesc Guitart; Xavier Ines; and Ana Pavicevic.

I want to thank Joan Soto, the photographer, for the experience and professionalism demonstrated in the images of this book; for the patience and dedication it took to make the extraordinary quality of this book possible; and for having taught me to see and understand the different renderings of an image.

Thanks goes to Parramón Publishers and its team of professionals who worked on this book, and especially to the editing director, María Fernanda Canal, for having trusted in its success.

I would also like to thank my wife and two children for their patience during the past year.

Carles Codina

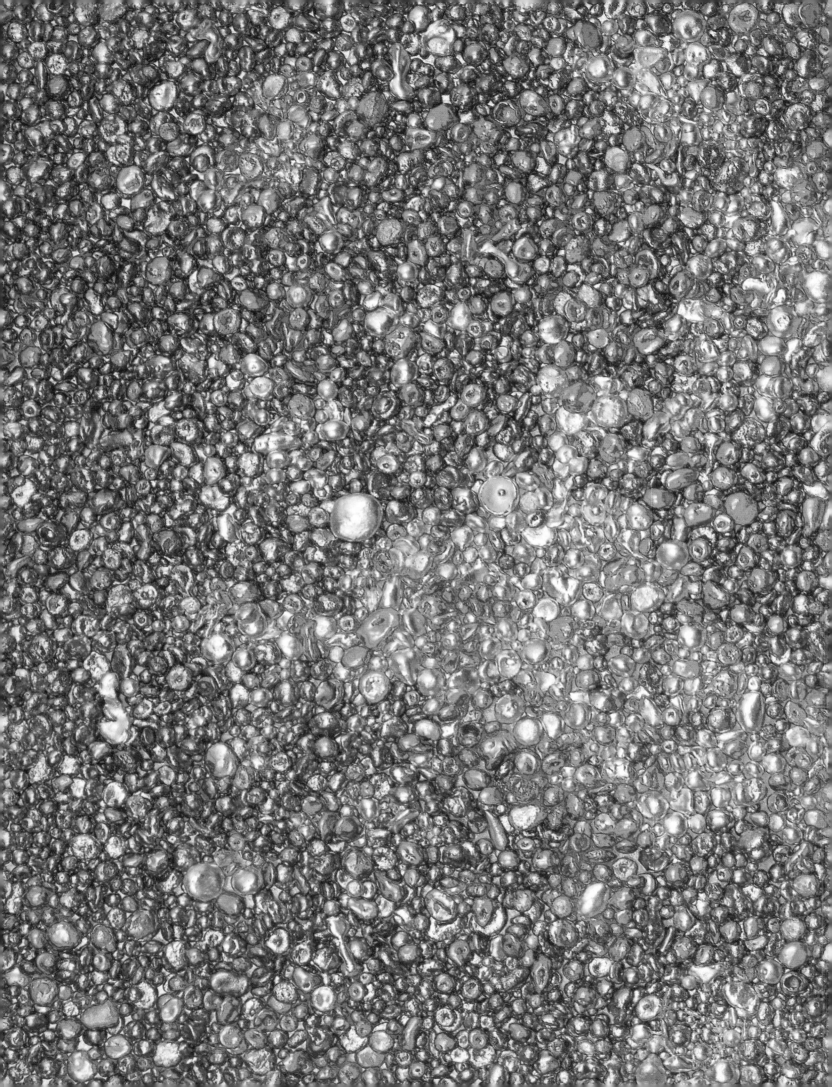